A NAZI LEGACY

A NAZI LEGACY
Depositing, Transgenerational Transmission, Dissociation, and Remembering Through Action

Vamık D. Volkan

LONDON AND NEW YORK

First published 2015 by Karnac Books Ltd.

Published 2018 by Routledge
2 Park Square, Milton Park, Abingdon, Oxon OX14 4RN
711 Third Avenue, New York, NY 10017, USA

Routledge is an imprint of the Taylor & Francis Group, an informa business

Copyright © 2015 to Vamık D. Volkan

The rights of Vamık D. Volkan to be identified as the author of this work have been asserted in accordance with §§ 77 and 78 of the Copyright Design and Patents Act 1988.

All rights reserved. No part of this book may be reprinted or reproduced or utilised in any form or by any electronic, mechanical, or other means, now known or hereafter invented, including photocopying and recording, or in any information storage or retrieval system, without permission in writing from the publishers.

Notice:
Product or corporate names may be trademarks or registered trademarks, and are used only for identification and explanation without intent to infringe.

British Library Cataloguing in Publication Data

A C.I.P. for this book is available from the British Library

ISBN-13: 9781782203704 (pbk)

Typeset by Medlar Publishing Solutions Pvt Ltd, India

CONTENTS

ABOUT THE AUTHOR	vii
PREFACE by Emily Kuriloff	ix
INTRODUCTION	xiii
CHAPTER ONE The impact of the Third Reich: The end of "silence" in psychoanalysis	1
CHAPTER TWO Victor: A man who lived in two different worlds	15
CHAPTER THREE A look at narcissism, splitting, depositing, dissociation, and encapsulation	23
CHAPTER FOUR The "Firefighter"	35

CHAPTER FIVE
A dead old man whose heart kept beating 43

CHAPTER SIX
The T4 euthanasia programme 49

CHAPTER SEVEN
Locked-up letters 53

CHAPTER EIGHT
Let there be oxygen 61

CHAPTER NINE
Legal redress and the psychology of remembering through actions 69

CHAPTER TEN
Photography, maggots, and jumping over a barbed wire fence 77

CHAPTER ELEVEN
Searching for and finding a new life 83

CHAPTER TWELVE
Another look at identification, depositing, and transgenerational transmission 91

REFERENCES 101

INDEX 111

ABOUT THE AUTHOR

Vamık D. Volkan, MD, is an emeritus professor of psychiatry at the University of Virginia School of Medicine, Charlottesville, Virginia, and an emeritus training and supervising psychoanalyst at the Washington Psychoanalytic Institute, Washington, DC. He served as the medical director of the University of Virginia's Blue Ridge Hospital and as director of the University of Virginia's Center for the Study of Mind and Human Interaction. He is a past president of the International Society of Political Psychology, the Virginia Psychoanalytic Society, the Turkish-American Neuropsychiatric Association, and the American College of Psychoanalysts. He holds honorary doctorate degrees from Kuopio University, Finland (now University of Eastern Finland); from Ankara University, Turkey; and from Eastern Psychoanalytical University, St. Petersburg, Russia. He served as a member of the Carter Center's International Negotiation Network, headed by former president Jimmy Carter. He was a visiting professor of law, Harvard University, Boston, Massachusetts, and a visiting professor of political science, University of Vienna, Vienna, Austria and Bahçeşehir University, Istanbul, Turkey. He was a temporary consultant to the World Health Organization in Albania and Macedonia; and a Fulbright Scholar in Austria. He has received many national or international awards including the Sigmund

Freud Award given by the city of Vienna in collaboration with the World Council of Psychotherapy. He was nominated in 2004–2006 and in 2014 for the Nobel Peace Prize for examining conflicts between opposing large groups, carrying out projects in various trouble spots in the world, and developing psychopolitical theories. Letters of support were sent from twenty-seven countries. At present he is the president of International Dialogue Initiative, a nonprofit organisation that brings together unofficial representatives from various parts of the world, including Israel, Iran, Turkey, West Bank, Russia, Germany, Great Britain, and the United States, to examine world affairs from a psychopolitical angle. He is the author, co-author, editor, or co-editor of dozens of books and has served on the editorial boards of sixteen national and international professional journals. He lectures internationally.

PREFACE

A psychoanalytic legacy: Vamık Volkan in action

Emily Kuriloff

As early as 1979, when external reality was viewed in psychoanalysis as but a signpost to an irreducible intrapsychic bedrock, the pioneering Vamık Volkan—a Turkish Cypriot—recognised the ways in which hate, destruction, and death in his homeland essentially transformed everyone (Volkan, 1979). But that was only the beginning of a bevy of influential publications. How global, local, and familial trauma impacts psychic life has taken Volkan around the globe and through the mind ever since, and, in this volume, across three generations in pre- and post-Nazi Germany.

The culture of psychoanalysis itself has suffered its own traumas and wars—acute and internecine—and Volkan's inviting me to write a preface to his newest work may reflect the evolution of these conflicts. Why do I say as much? My interpersonal psychoanalytic training downplayed the rich focus on the inner life that this leader in the field clearly honours in all of his writing. Yet many of my equally influential teachers not only rejected any a priori psychic structure and function, but went as far as to claim that the quality of an individual's relationships—cultural and familial—determined the essence of a dynamic, even mercurial, mind.

Freud, it must be said, never abandoned the impact of relatedness and environment in his evolving notions, even as he pioneered a new model of mind. I have, however, written elsewhere (Kuriloff, 2014) about the ways in which *post*-war psychoanalytic theory, dominated by refugees from the Shoah, tended to reify otherwise supple ideas of the mentor who triumphed in a culture suddenly turned genocidal. At the same time that the intrapsychic became more inviolable, the post-war theorist's traumatic past, and thus trauma in general, were similarly downplayed, perhaps so that the refugees could rebuild and grow what was to become its own rich tradition. Because, ironically, it is current events that are most distant from self-reflexivity, it took many years after the liberation of Auschwitz for analysts to hold both the intrapsychic and the interpersonal in their conceptions and praxis. Volkan's invitation to write this preface may not only reflect the prescience with which he has long acknowledged the impact of trauma, but also a recent end to the war after the war, a sea change that provides an opportunity for us to share and expand our points of view.

In keeping with this theme, I shall focus on Volkan's felicitous term "depositing" in his understanding of intergenerational transmission of trauma. This neologism, it seems to me, elegantly describes a particular and quintessentially interpersonal process that shapes the core of intrapsychic life. What do I mean by this? Let me begin with Volkan's own definition. He writes:

> In depositing, the adult person is the active partner who plants his specific images into the developing self-representation of the child. In other words, the adult person uses the child (mostly unconsciously) as a permanent reservoir for certain self- and other images belonging to that adult and initiates the child's certain psychological tasks linked to these transferred images. The experiences that created these mental images in the adult are not accessible to the child. Yet, those mental images are pushed into the child without the experiential/contextual framework that created them. Melanie Klein's (1946) "projective identification" can explain such a process. However, I wish to use the term "depositing" to illustrate how parenting individuals create a psychological DNA in the child. (p. 28 in this book)

Volkan suggests that particular qualities of relatedness in the family are nothing less than the building blocks of psychic structure, an individual's "psychological DNA". That is, a traumatised parent experiences the child as but an extension, a receptacle, for unwanted affect, unable to honour him or her as a subject with a unique mind and experience. The child is, in effect, deprived of a mind, unable to mentalise, or reflect on, and thus regulate, feeling states (Fonagy, Gyorgy, Jurist, & Target, 2003). Volkan continues to hone the impact of his concept of "depositing" by distinguishing it from identification, which can only happen when a parent does, in fact, acknowledge the child's separate subjectivity. Identification involves the parent's providing a mirroring function that reflects the child's unique experience and agency, all required for active identification and, finally, internalisation of the other.

We become intimately familiar with the failure to be an active subject, the damage done by "depositing", as we read this book's story of the grandson of the Nazi, who, as but one glaring example, neither recalls his own bizarre behaviours during sleep-like states, nor has any awareness that these dissociated episodes evoke his grandfather's murderous history. These details are deposited into the patient by his parents, and are stories that remain unformulated, unmentalised, but concretised, enacted by the patient in dangerous and disruptive ways.

Finally, this transformative story not only illustrates the impact of trauma across generations in a relational psychoanalytic process between analyst and analysand that itself repeats and reveals the patient's experience, but, in addition, we learn about the *supervisory* psychoanalytic process. Indeed, the communication between the patient's analyst, Dr. Adeline, and the author/analytic supervisor, Dr. Volkan, reflects many aspects of the mirroring and identification, and thus the internalisation, that allows for symbolic meaning and memory in trauma work. Volkan's non-directive, and yet evocative, style includes the reader in the literal and figurative long distance, and yet describes the affectively alive interaction between three people struggling to witness, to feel, and to formulate what has been a privately unbearable, unformulated experience.

Emily A. Kuriloff is a training and supervising analyst at The William Alanson White Institute in New York, where she is also the director of clinical education. She is the special issues editor for the journal Contemporary Psychoanalysis, and its former book review editor. Dr. Kuriloff is the author of numerous journal articles exploring the interpersonal psychoanalytic tradition and comparative models of technique and therapeutic action.

References

Fonagy, P., Gyorgy, G., Jurist, E. L., & Target, M. (2003). *Affect Regulation, Mentalization, and the Development of the Self*. London: Karnac.

Kuriloff, E. (2014). *Contemporary Psychoanalysis and the Legacy of the Third Reich: History, Memory, Tradition*. New York & London: Routledge.

Volkan, V. (1979). *Cyprus: War and Adaptation: A Psychoanalytic History of Two Ethnic Groups in Conflict*. Charlottesville, VA: University of Virginia Press.

INTRODUCTION

The primary aim of this book is to tell the story of the grandson of a high-level Nazi SS officer, an officer who had been actively involved in a programme aimed at the extermination of many innocent people. The book illustrates the consequences of transgenerational transmission of self- and object images with associated psychological tasks, the development of an encapsulated dissociated self, and psychopathology remembered through actions. It describes transference-countertransference difficulties when the relationship between the analysand and the analyst becomes linked to painful traumatic historical events. I named the patient "Victor" and his psychoanalyst "Adeline".

I first met Dr. Adeline about a decade before she started to work with Victor, when I was invited to give a speech on the treatment of so-called "difficult patients" in a German city where she lived. She was a member of the board of the institution that had arranged and sponsored my visit, and the day after my speech she was given the task of showing me a town near a castle outside of her city, a tourist destination. On our way to the castle she told me about one of her patients, a male nurse. His problem was "shyness" and anxiety around other nurses at the hospital where he worked because he did not want them to know that he was originally from the former East Germany. Listening to Dr. Adeline I heard about the lingering "mental division" of unified Germany, at least in some individuals' minds, years after reunification had taken place. This male nurse was married to a female nurse who was born in the former West Germany, but whose father, with his new wife, had come to Germany from a conservative village in Anatolia decades earlier as a guest worker. The nurse and his wife had a six-year-old daughter whose maternal grandparents called her by her Turkish middle name instead of the German name that she used in public. The patient's in-laws were pressuring their daughter to raise her child according to Anatolian traditions. This situation provided another reason for the patient's "shyness" around his fellow hospital workers from the former West Germany. Dr. Adeline was not familiar with Turkish and Middle Eastern cultural customs and knew that I was a Cypriot Turk who graduated from a medical school in Turkey before moving to the United States. In order to better understand her patient's relationship with his Turkish-German in-laws, as well as with his wife, Dr. Adeline and I consulted by phone after I returned to the United States. Our regular once- or twice-a-month phone calls continued for over two years until she and her patient successfully finished treatment.

Years later I received a letter from Dr. Adeline. She reminded me of our lunch at the centre of the beautiful town overlooking the lake after our visit to the nearby castle. She stated that a man from this town, twelve years younger than she, had come to see her and had been lying on her couch three times a week for the last five months. She briefly described this man Victor's main symptom—he woke up in the early morning and entered another mental state for about four hours. She was aware that he was a "difficult patient" and told me how she had not been able to develop a therapeutic alliance with him. She asked me if she could call me from Germany again for consultation. I agreed, and she called me every other week for some months until we began making sense of why Victor was behaving on the couch as if he was his own psychoanalyst while keeping Dr. Adeline as if she was an observer of his "self-analysis". Although I would not become a "regular" supervisor for Victor's psychoanalysis, throughout many years, on and off, Dr. Adeline continued to get in touch with me by phone or email to consult about her work with Victor, or simply to inform me of new developments in his case. Whenever we met at international psychoanalytic gatherings we found time to sit down and have face-to-face talks about her analysand. It took nearly three years before Dr. Adeline and I fully realised how the image of Victor's Nazi grandfather played the key role in his grandson's psychopathology.

Papers and books by psychoanalysts detailing stories of Jewish survivors of the Holocaust as well as survivors' children and grandchildren are many; I will make references to some of them in this book. While psychoanalysts have contributed a great deal to the psychology of the Nazis and written psychobiographies of some Nazi leaders, including psychobiographies of Adolf Hitler (see, for example, Dorpat, 2002; Langer, 1972; Redlich, 1998), detailed psychoanalytic examinations of offspring of important Nazi perpetrators *on a psychoanalyst's couch* are rare.

Last year Dr. Adeline expressed her wish to make a record of Victor's case. She felt that it was a most clear symbolic representation of the Third Reich's transgenerational history. Obviously not every German person with a criminal Nazi ancestor develops psychopathology. Also, German society in general, after the Third Reich, has developed a very different large-group identity and new shared sentiments. Nevertheless, Dr. Adeline, I noticed, felt that telling Victor's story was her societal duty. It had been my custom to keep notes whenever I supervised younger psychoanalysts or consulted with colleagues, and I had kept records of my consultations with Dr. Adeline. She knew my custom and asked me if I would join her in writing Victor's case. After hearing my willingness to do so, she expressed that only I, as a close outsider observer, should tell Victor's story. Doing so would greatly help to protect Victor's identity. I agreed to write this story with her help. To protect Victor's real identity further, I have made changes in Victor's external world in some areas that, I believe, will not affect my description of his internal world and behaviour patterns.

I am dedicating this book to Dr. Adeline with my deepest appreciation for her internal struggles while analysing Victor and her dedication to our profession. She read the manuscript of this book before its publication and approved it.

CHAPTER ONE

The impact of the Third Reich: The end of "silence" in psychoanalysis

In June 1988 an important international conference entitled "Persistent shadows of the Holocaust: The meaning to those not directly affected" took place at the Sigmund Freud Center at the Hebrew University in Jerusalem. Two Israeli (Jewish) psychoanalysts, a German psychoanalyst, an American Jewish psychoanalyst, and an American non-Jewish psychoanalyst gave speeches and described their personal experiences and theoretical views related to the Holocaust. The audience of about 120 was composed of psychoanalysts, teachers, and people from other backgrounds. They were citizens of many countries including Israel, Germany, the United States, Australia, Holland, Sweden, and Switzerland and North African and Middle Eastern Sephardic Jews who had experienced no direct contact with the Holocaust. Twelve well-known psychoanalysts from Israel, Germany, and the United States led discussion groups that followed the four presentations, and still other distinguished psychoanalysts from different countries functioned as discussants. Significant data on the impact of the Holocaust on the general public, including those who were not directly affected, and difficulties in mourning over many kinds of losses, came to light. The question, "How can the recurrence of an event like the Holocaust in our world be prevented?" was asked again and again (Moses, 1993).

I was the American non-Jewish psychoanalyst who presented a paper at this meeting. At the beginning of my speech I gave brief information about my background, informing everyone in the audience that I was born to Turkish Muslim parents in Cyprus and graduated from Ankara Medical School in Turkey before immigrating to the United States in 1957 and becoming an American citizen a few years later. Main protagonists at this international meeting were Jewish and German psychoanalysts. This was the first time that I learned about German psychoanalysts' reactions to the impact of the Holocaust and how it affected them and their patients.

During the Cold War, the Berlin Wall stood as the ultimate symbol of the physical as well as psychological border between the East and the West. As a *psychological* border, the Berlin Wall, during the years when it was experienced as stable, allowed the societies on either side to effectively externalise, project, and displace their shared unwanted self- or object images, thoughts, and affects on to the other side without feeling anxiety that these elements would be returned to them (Volkan, 2003). Donald Winnicott (1969) reminded us that, while the Berlin Wall, a man-made barricade, was unsightly and completely disassociated from "beauty", without it there would have been a war in the 1960s. Winnicott went on to further elucidate the beneficial aspect of the Wall. He argued that a dividing line between opposing forces at its worst postpones conflict and at its best holds opposing forces apart for long periods of time so that people may "play" and pursue the arts of peace. The arts of peace belong to the temporary success of a dividing line between opposing forces, the lull between times when the wall ceases to segregate good and bad (Winnicott, 1969).

The Berlin Wall divided East from West Germany from 1961 to 1989, and its demolition, which began in the summer of 1990, was completed in 1992. The German Reunification Treaty was signed on 31 August 1990. After the border between East and West Germany was opened, German psychoanalyst Gabriele Ast and I started a project to examine how Germans, from both sides, were reacting to meeting one another after their forty-year separation. We anticipated that opening the border and imagining a unified Germany would induce anxiety as two separate, four-decades-long large-group identities were being lost, and that this anxiety might linger for years (Ast, 1991; Volkan, 1990a, 2013). We began to conduct long psychoanalytic interviews with people from both the former East Germany and the former West Germany and found data supporting our thesis. Here are two examples:

Sabine from the former West Germany in her late twenties was undergoing her personal analysis as part of her psychoanalytic training at the time of reunification. The reunification was the day residue for her dream in which people were standing in an open truck. She told me: "When I saw the truck I knew it was a picture from the Nazi era, of Jews being deported to Auschwitz. I felt very guilty for coming up with this picture". She explained that the reunification pleased her in many ways, but also instilled the fear that it would "recreate the murderer, the monster" (Nazis, Hitler) that perpetuated so many horrors. She and her analyst of Jewish origin would speak of the Holocaust but could not fully explore this topic to analyse her fantasies and affects related to the Third Reich.

Before the reunification Hans, a law student from the former East Germany, helped his parents build a house on a hill overlooking a lake. In his dream following the reunification, a wealthy man builds a much larger house on the same hill. This man then tells Hans and his family to move out of their newly built home because it obstructs his view of the lake. As consolation, the wealthy man offers the second floor of his house to the family, and though Hans' parents quarrel with their "landlord", the rich man wins in the end. In the dream, the newly built house explodes as soon as Hans and his family move in with the wealthy "landlord". Hans' associations to this dream, apart from those relating to divisions within his childhood family, were to the German reunification. Hans knew that the wealthy neighbour in the dream represented West Germany. His experiences with early emotional and physical divisions in his family (between his mother and father and between his mother and grandmother) were condensed in the country's division between East and West. While the luxury of the rich man's larger house was appealing to Hans, his old self (his family's house) in the German Democratic Republic was threatened and disappearing. He spoke of how he was paralysed for half an hour and felt completely numb on the night of the official German reunification. He noted a military confrontation was eliminated, but he was overwhelmed by anxiety that, with the two sides now united, the aggressive representations—including Third Reich images—symbolised by West Germany would destroy innocent representations symbolised by East Germany.

Our initial findings showed that certain images related to the Third Reich and the Holocaust that individuals did not wish to own and their associated affects and fantasies had been externalised, projected, and displaced from one side of the border to the other. Our project was unfortunately truncated due to insufficient funds after Dr. Ast and I had conducted only twenty-one interviews. After the fall of the Berlin Wall I was a guest of the German Psychoanalytic Society's annual meeting and was able to observe how some psychoanalysts from West Germany related in a somewhat degrading manner to colleagues from East Germany who were not yet officially accepted as psychoanalysts by the International Psychoanalytic Association. Dr. Ast's and my initial findings and my observations at the German Psychoanalytic meeting were supported by other researchers who investigated the psychology of German reunification. For example, in separate studies Dieter Ohlmeier (1991), Hans-Joachim Maaz (1991), Adam Weisberger (1995), and Irene Misselwitz (2003) declared that the reunification of Germany was not only a major political change, but was also a major psychological event, prompting a new wave of renegotiations with the Nazi past. Maaz wrote that the division of Germany resulted in each side regarding the other as either nefarious capitalists, imperialists, and revanchists or dangerous communists and Bolshevists (Maaz, 1991).

In June 1990, when the official discussions for the signing of German reunification were taking place, another international conference, this one titled "Children of war", convened, again at the Sigmund Freud Center at the Hebrew University. It was sponsored by the Israel Psychoanalytic Society, The World Federation for Mental Health, and Harvard University's Department of Psychiatry. Before this meeting I had observed and interviewed children at Beit Atfal al-Sumud, a home for orphaned Palestinian children in Tunis that housed fifty-seven boys and girls (Volkan, 1990b, 2014a). Once more I was a speaker at an international meeting at the Sigmund Freud Center and this time I described my findings from Beit Atfal al-Sumud. At this point, Dr. Ast's and my project in Germany concerning the psychological consequences of the border opening between East and West Germany was under way, so after giving my speech I began looking for German participants at the meeting to interview. I met Liliane Opher-Cohn, a Jewish-German child-psychotherapist. Her parents were survivors of the Holocaust, and she was preoccupied with what it meant to be Jewish. We spoke about the Third Reich-related issues appearing in patients' sessions in Germany. She told me that these issues were not likely to surface in the official world of psychotherapy and that there was still a "silence" around this topic.

In a sense it was incorrect to refer to a silence concerning the Holocaust in Germany. After all, the German government has repeatedly acknowledged the crimes of the Nazis in the form of financial compensation, and publications, monuments, and artistic works have anatomised the period of the Third Reich. In 1970, Chancellor Willy Brandt's falling on his knees before a monument to the victims of the Warsaw Ghetto uprising would become a symbol of asking for forgiveness in international relationships. But rather than this kind of public declaration, Liliane Opher-Cohn and I were speaking of another kind of silence: the use of psychological mechanisms—ranging from intellectualisation and denial to splitting and dissociation—that protect self-esteem by establishing emotional distance from aspects of the Holocaust and its transgenerational intrapsychic ramifications. By the time I met Liliane Opher-Cohn, German-speaking psychoanalysts had already reported (or would later report) their difficulties in "hearing" Nazi-related influences in their German and Jewish patients (Eckstaedt, 1989; Grubrich-Simitis, 1979; Jokl, 1997; Streeck-Fischer, 1999; Volkan, Ast, & Greer, 2002).

After returning to Germany from Jerusalem, Liliane Opher-Cohn began a process to investigate the psychology of the transgenerational consequences of the Holocaust for the children of the survivors as well as the perpetrators. She was interested in breaking the "silence" of the clinical setting and within the society. Her unbending will led to the formation, in July 1995, of an organisation called *Psychotherapeutischer Arbeitskreis für Betroffene des Holocaust, PAKH e.V.* (Psychotherapeutic study group of persons affected by the Holocaust). Most of PAKH's founders, ten individuals, were psychoanalytic psychotherapists. Four of them were Jewish-Germans. Besides finding ways to talk about Holocaust-related topics while conducting psychotherapy, PAKH's purpose was to work, through *Aufklärung* (enlightenment), against neglecting the acknowledgment of persecution and genocide under National Socialism and to utilise psychoanalytic understanding of human nature to prevent xenophobia and anti-Semitism in Germany. PAKH associated itself with the Institute of Psychosomatic and Psychotherapy at the University of Cologne. This gave PAKH access to scientific work. In 2007, its name was changed to *Arbeitskreis für intergenerationelle Folgen des Holocaust, ehem. PAKH e.V.* (Study group for intergenerational consequences of the Holocaust).

Since they believed that the impact of World War II and the Holocaust on the offspring of survivors and perpetrators had not been properly examined in Germany by psychotherapists and psychoanalysts, the founders of PAKH planned to have an international symposium to deal with the "silence". They faced many difficulties, major ones being the relationships among themselves. Starting in February 1997 I met with this group, several full days each time, on four occasions. I describe my meetings with them in detail elsewhere (Volkan, Ast, & Greer, 2002), but in summary, the members of the PAKH core group were people with similar interests, not enemies. However, their German and Jewish parents, grandparents, and relatives had lived in completely different circumstances. They had been enemies, victims, and perpetrators, and the next generation had carried forward this ill-starred heritage on both conscious and unconscious levels. Although half a century had passed since the Nazi period, they carried within themselves the inexpressible trauma of the war and of annihilation. After Germans and Jewish-German founders of PAKH had worked through their major obstacles against a joint project, PAKH's international symposium took place in Düsseldorf in August 1998. It was named *Das Ende der Sprachlosigkeit?* (End of speechlessness?) (Opher-Cohn, Pfäfflin, Sonntag, Klose, & Pogany-Wnendt, 2000). I have kept in contact with PAKH members over many years and joined them again during the tenth anniversary of the establishment of their organisation. I am aware of their expanding vision and influence, including their work with scholars in South Africa who are finding ways to tame the impact of Apartheid (Gobodo-Madikizela & Van der Merwe, 2009).

Writing about the "silence" experienced among German psychoanalysts and psychotherapists while treating German patients is not complete without noting a similar "silence" among psychoanalysts elsewhere as they worked with Jewish survivors of the Holocaust. Let me begin by making a reference to "silence" in Israel: after World War II ended, Paul Friedman from the United States came to Cyprus, my birthplace, which was then a British colony and examined many survivors—adults as well as children—who were being held at a detention center for displaced persons who had sought "illegal" entry into Palestine. He published a paper and referred to the "deeper psychodynamics of the handful of people who emerged from the camps after liberation" (Friedman, 1949, p. 601). But, in general, attention to "deeper psychodynamics" was avoided. On 29 November 1947 the United Nations Assembly officially created Israel. After their arrival in Israel, many survivors were treated for depression and other mental disorders in psychiatric hospitals. Many of these patients' official files did not even mention that they were Holocaust victims (Volkan, Ast, & Greer, 2002). Judith Stern (2001) reminded us that half of the Jewish population in Palestine in 1945 had come between 1933 and 1939, and they had no direct experience of the Holocaust. She added that after the successful struggle to establish the State of Israel, no image could have been more threatening to the new polity's myth of the fighting and ultimately successful hero, the *Sabra* (Israeli Jews born in Israel proper, Gaza, and the West Bank), than that of the Holocaust survivor. A decade after Paul Friedman's study, a cascade of psychoanalytic investigations of the internal worlds of Jewish survivors appeared in the psychoanalytic literature. William Niederland (1961, 1968) coined the term "survivor syndrome" and Robert Lifton (1968) observed that survivors of Hiroshima had much in common with the survivors of the Nazi camps. Niederland's work, however, to a great extent led to the presumption that every survivor was obliged to develop psychopathology. It is well known that Niederland interviewed thousands of survivors with the aim of helping them receive reparation from the German government. The German restitution laws necessitated psychiatric examination of thousands of survivors of the Holocaust who were then living in the United States. Niederland's task most likely played a role in his inclination to portray all survivors whom he interviewed as damaged. In 1968 a meeting took place at Wayne State University to examine the late sequelae of massive psychic trauma. It was organised by Henry Krystal, himself a survivor. Like Niederland he had conducted thousands of interviews with other survivors and described the inability to enjoy oneself after liberation and the incredible difficulty in finding one's post-liberation identity. William Niederland was the key contributor at the Wayne State University gathering. Niederland's, Krystal's, and the other twelve contributors' findings created a notion that "survivor syndrome" existed in any survivor of the Holocaust. The most common psychiatric clinical picture of this syndrome included chronic reactive depression, guilt complex, psychosomatic and hypochondrial symptoms, anxiety, agitation, severe personality changes, and psychotic expressions (Krystal, 1968). By 1970, psychoanalytic workshops on survivors' children began to take place and psychoanalysts' observations on the transgenerational transmission of the Holocaust trauma expanded (Sonnenberg, 1974). Under different names, such as "transgenerational transposition" (Kestenberg,1982),"depositing" (Volkan,1987;Volkan,Ast,&Greer,2002),

"ancestor syndrome" (Schützenberger, 1998), or "telescoping of generations" (Faimberg, 2005), the phenomenon of offspring's reactions to their ancestor's trauma became part of psychoanalytic work.

Decades later, psychoanalysts in the United States (for example, see Kuriloff, 2013; Laub & Auerhahn, 1993; Laub & Podell, 1995) and Israel (for example, see Kogan, 2007) would recognise many types of adaptations, including creative adaptations that survivors and their offspring made to their massive psychic and physical trauma. Some psychoanalysts who were directly affected by the Holocaust also ended their "silence", decades after the end of World War II, and wrote movingly about their experiences. I am most familiar with two of these stories (Ornstein, 2004; Parens, 2004). About the creative response to the Holocaust among Jewish persons Kogan (2007) writes:

> Creative activity that involves the legacy of the Holocaust (as we often see in cases of the Holocaust survivors' children) is … a quest for mastery and redemption. By appearing in the transitional space between reenactment and representation, creative activity ultimately allows the patient to be in touch with mourning and enables its working through. It affirms the forces of life, thus overcoming the silence and death. As an act of imagination, it is a path to hope and a profound beginning. (p. 122)

In spite of many psychodynamic studies, workshops, papers, and presentations on Holocaust survivors and their offspring, the "silence" *in the clinical setting* continued. Rafael Moses (1984), Peter Loewenberg (1991), Leo Rangell (2003), and Ira Brenner (2004) remind us that some aspects of external historical events, especially the Holocaust, induce anxiety. For example, in the United States Harold Blum (1985) describes a Jewish patient who came to him for reanalysis and informs us that the patient's first analyst, who was also Jewish, failed to "hear" their large group's shared trauma at the hands of the Nazis in his patient's material. As a consequence, mutually sanctioned silence and denial pervaded the entire analytic experience, leaving unanalysed residues of the Holocaust in the patient's symptoms. Emily Kuriloff (2013) illustrated how the Holocaust affected psychoanalytic theory and the clinical approach to patients, especially survivors.

There is another reason for this "silence". This is the classical psychoanalytic tradition of putting the influence of external events in the shadows while conducting treatment. It is true that, beginning with Sigmund Freud, psychoanalysts have ventured beyond the couch and written about myths, religions, wars, and related topics. Nevertheless, until a few decades ago psychoanalysts did not focus much on how external events impacted the psychopathology of individuals they were treating. They followed the tradition that originated with Freud's giving up the seduction theory in his early efforts to develop psychoanalytic theories (Freud, 1905). The idea of the sexual seduction of children coming from the external world was relinquished in favour of the belief that stimuli that came from the child's own wishes and fantasies resulted in the formation of psychopathology. Thus, classical psychoanalysis placed less emphasis on the impact of *actual* seduction coming from the external world on the developing child's psyche, and this was generalised to include de-emphasis on the psychic impact of external events.

Freud was aware of "war neurosis". After World War I ended, in Beyond the Pleasure Principle, he wrote that he was not aware "that patients suffering from traumatic neurosis are much occupied in their waking lives with memories of their accident. Perhaps they are more concerned with not thinking of it. Anyone who accepts it as something self-evident that their dreams should put them back at night into the situation that caused them to fall ill has misunderstood the nature of dreams" (Freud, 1920, p. 13). A few years later he stated that war neuroses "opened the eyes of the medical profession to the importance of psychogenesis in neurotic disturbances, and some of our psychological conceptions, such as the 'gain from illness' and the 'flight into illness', quickly became popular" (Freud, 1925, p. 54). However, in general, the focus in the clinical setting was on exploring psychic reality only: an analysand's unconscious conflicts, resistances against exploring them, development of transference neurosis, and its resolution. The emphasis on the unconscious, to a great extent, screened out the influence of external events and traumas associated with those events, especially when the patient was not an active player in an external event taking place in his or her neighbourhood, community, ethnic group, or nation.

A major dispute evolved between Freud and Sándor Ferenczi about the influence of actual trauma, actual sexual abuse, on individuals' internal worlds (Falzeder & Brabant, 2000; Paláez, 2009; Rachman, 1997). In general, however, classical psychoanalysts continued to follow Freud's path in de-emphasising the role of traumatic external events, including those at the hand of the Other, in their psychoanalytic work with patients. This also, to a great extent, prevented them from being interested in examining societal traumas.

Freud left another legacy that discouraged his followers from pursuing political and diplomatic processes in their daily clinical practices and thus also traumas linked to such processes. In 1932 Albert Einstein wrote a letter to Freud and asked the following questions: "Is there any way of delivering mankind from the menace of war?" "How is it possible for [a small group with political power hunger] to bend the will of the majority, who stand to lose and suffer by a state of war, to the service of their ambitions?" and "Is it possible to control man's mental evolution so as to make him proof against the psychoses of hate and destructiveness?" (Freud, 1932, pp. 199–201). In his response to Einstein, Freud expressed little hope for an end to war and violence or the role of psychoanalysis in changing human behaviour beyond the individual level. Although Jacob Arlow (1973) later recognised some optimism in some of Freud's writings on this subject, Freud's pessimism about the role of psychoanalysis in major external traumatic events was mirrored during World War II by many psychoanalysts, including Melanie Klein who was introducing her own theories on the development of the human mind. For example, she did not pay attention to the war when she treated a ten-year-old boy named Richard in 1941 (Klein, 1961). During Richard's analysis, the terror of the Blitz under which Melanie Klein and Richard lived was not examined. There were exceptions. Psychoanalysts such as Edward Glower (1947), Franco Fornari (1966), Robert Waelder (1971), Alexander Mitscherlich and Margarete Mitscherlich (Mitscherlich, 1971; Mitscherlich & Mitscherlich, 1975) tried to open doors to such investigations.

I did my training analysis in the early 1960s in the United States, a time when ethnic conflict between Greek Cypriots and Turkish Cypriots was occurring in my birthplace. My roommate in Ankara when he and I were attending the Ankara University School of Medicine, Erol Mulla, was also from Cyprus and two years younger than I. In early 1957, just a few months after I came to the United States as a newly graduated physician, Erol, during a visit to Cyprus to see his ailing mother, was shot seven times by a Greek Cypriot terrorist. The killer's identity would never be officially released. In the 1960s my mother, father, sisters, and other family members in Cyprus were living in an enclave under subhuman conditions surrounded by Greek Cypriot and United Nations soldiers.

My analyst was Jewish. During my analysis what was happening in Cyprus and what was happening to my family members were not topics we explored. Was this because of my psychological condition? Perhaps I did not want to recognise and verbalise my guilt for being alive while my former roommate had been killed and for living in safety while the walls of my sisters' houses were scarred with bullet holes. Much later, after my analysis was over, I also wondered if exploring what was happening to my family members in Cyprus would have induced unpleasant thoughts and feelings about the Holocaust in my analyst. Was this his reason for keeping the tragic events happening on the island during my analysis outside his office? Decades later I realised that my "creative" response to the societal traumas that affected me was my main motivation for studying mourning (Volkan, 1972, 1981, 2014a; Volkan & Zintl, 1993) and later examining international relations from a psychoanalytic angle (Volkan, 1979, 2010, 2014b).

Ira Brenner was present during PAKH's "End of speechlessness?" meeting in Düsseldorf, and since then he has contributed significantly to our understanding of the consequences of massive trauma, especially the Holocaust, and the treatment of those suffering from these consequences (Brenner, 2001, 2004, 2014). In his foreword to the book *The Third Reich in the Unconscious* (Volkan, Ast, & Greer, 2002) Brenner described how he began his work in this area by becoming a member of the Group for the Psychoanalytic Study of the Effects of the Holocaust (Brenner, 2002). One of the co-chairpersons of this Group, Judith Kestenberg (1982), had already coined the term "transposition" to describe how survivor parents were transmitting their trauma unconsciously to their children. Brenner tells the story of one of his analysands, a Jewish man, who was entangled with the law and jailed at the very age that his father was during his hiding and escape from, and subsequent capture by, the Gestapo. Brenner presented this case to members of his group and to outsider psychoanalysts to illustrate how it was imperative for his analysand to pay attention to the link between his actions that put him in jail and his parent's Holocaust experience. Brenner tells the story of how a number of "very talented 'outsider' analysts" challenged him by arguing that "analysis deals with the realm of psychic reality only" and that Brenner and his colleagues "were introducing an unnecessary element that only 'muddied the waters' and was unnecessary for successful treatment" (Brenner, 2002, p. xiii).

However, at the time these "outsider" analysts were maintaining their opposition to including Holocaust-related psychological reactions in clinical work, there were already significant contributions by psychoanalysts illustrating the intertwining of internal and external worlds. For example, Michael Šebek (1992, 1994) studied societal responses to living under communism in Europe. Sudhir Kakar (1996) described the effects of Hindu-Muslim religious conflict in Hyderabad, India. Maurice Apprey (1993, 1998) focused on the influence of transgenerational transmission of trauma on African-Americans and their culture. Nancy Hollander (1997) explored events in South America. Salman Akhtar (1999) wrote about immigration and identity. However, "silence" in the psychoanalysts' office about Holocaust-related issues, as illustrated by Brenner, still persevered to some extent.

Ira Brenner's case presentation took place before 11 September 2001. It is fair to say that since that date the majority of psychoanalysts in the United States and other locations have given up the position of the "outsider analysts" who were present at Ira Brenner's case presentation, and they have begun to consider the intertwining of external and internal worlds in their patients' treatment processes. After 11 September 2001 the International Psychoanalytic Association (IPA) formed the Terror and Terrorism Study Group. Norwegian psychoanalyst Sverre Varvin chaired this study group, which lasted for several years (Varvin & Volkan, 2003). The IPA also established a committee in the United Nations. The theme of the 44th Annual Meeting of the IPA in Rio de Janeiro in the summer of 2005 was "trauma", including trauma due to historical events. In 2011, during the plenary lecture at the American Psychoanalytic Association's Winter Meeting, outgoing president Prudence Gourguechon urged the members of the association to show their faces in areas already in the public eye. She stated that if psychoanalysts do not attempt to explain the causality of disturbing events and to provide professional information about human behaviour, statements by others with less knowledge on such matters will prevail. Nancy Hollander looked at the United States after 11 September 2001 (Hollander, 2010), and other psychoanalysts examined the impact of other massive traumas and the intertwining of external and internal worlds. In only a few examples of such studies, Mitch Elliott, Kenneth Bishop, and Paul Stokes (2004), and John Alderdice (2007, 2010) examined the situation in Northern Ireland. Shmuel Erlich (2010) explored the terrorist mind. Gerard Fromm (2011) edited a book on transmissions of the impact of trauma from generation to generation. Bruno Boccara (2014) opened a door to applying psychoanalytically informed thinking to economic and social transformations.

During my decades-long work in international relations I wrote about the influence that shared images of specific historical events during ancestors' times—I called them "chosen traumas" or "chosen glories"—have on societies. Such shared images become most significant "identity markers" for ethnic, national, religious, or political ideological large groups—tens, thousands, or millions of people who share the same language, sentiments, nursery rhythms, language, food, dances, and other things. When a present-day conflict begins with current enemies, "chosen glories" and "chosen traumas" are reactivated along with entitlement ideologies. Entitlement ideologies refer to a shared sense of entitlement to recover what was lost in reality and fantasy during the collective trauma that evolved as a chosen trauma. Or they refer to the mythologised birth of a large group, a process which later generations idealise. They deny difficulties and losses that occurred during the event, and imagine their large group as if it were composed of persons belonging to a superior species. Holding on to an entitlement ideology primarily reflects a complication in large-group mourning, an attempt both to deny losses as well as a wish to recover them, a narcissistic reorganisation accompanied by "bad" prejudice for the Other. The reactivation of "chosen glories" and "chosen traumas", along with entitlement ideologies within a society, creates a "time collapse": feelings, perceptions, fears, prejudices, and wishes connected with such "identity markers" become intertwined with feelings and thoughts about the current enemy. This magnifies dangers, confuses reality, and leads to "magical thinking", thus complicating attempts toward peaceful solutions (Volkan, 1988, 1997, 2004a, 2006a, 2013, 2014b). My findings in large-group psychology led me to notice more clearly how historical events and traumas play a role in structuring individuals' personal psychology throughout generations (Volkan, 2014c; Volkan & Fowler, 2009).

My observations in Germany around the period when the Berlin Wall fell, my involvement with PAKH, and my appearing at professional meetings held in Germany gave me an opportunity to meet many younger German psychoanalytic colleagues, including Dr. Adeline. Throughout recent decades a number of these colleagues have consulted with me about their work with their analysands. In this way, I continued to have a close look at how German psychoanalysts are bringing Third Reich-related traumatic events into the psychoanalytic process. I also wish to repeat that obviously not every German on a psychoanalyst's couch has a major problem or psychopathology intimately related to his or her ancestors' involvement in National Socialism. Nevertheless, even though at the present time my German colleagues are more aware of this issue, I notice that the "silence" still appears in the treatment of some individuals. Now I will return to Victor's case, where "silence" was present for some time.

CHAPTER TWO

Victor: A man who lived in two different worlds

One day Dr. Adeline received a telephone call from a psychoanalyst living and working in another German city. After introducing himself, the caller stated that he had recently read a paper by Dr. Adeline on early childhood traumas and their consequences. He was impressed by Dr. Adeline's case report and theoretical ideas and was calling to refer to her a patient, his niece's boyfriend, since this individual lived in a small town just outside in the city where Dr. Adeline worked. The caller's niece had come to see him recently and ask for his help for her boyfriend who had a bizarre symptom. Whenever she spent nights with him she noticed that sometime after midnight he would wake up suddenly, often shaking her and waking her up too. He would say bizarre things, such as "We need to find a way to get out of here right away" and do bizarre things, such as trying to remove the mattress from the bed and push it out of the window. He would notice how fast his heart was beating and fear that his heart muscles might be damaged. She would try to calm him down, but he would not respond and he appeared to remain in another world, sometimes for several hours, before he could return to bed and fall asleep. The next day he would seem normal and happy. The psychoanalyst had never met Victor, but had his permission to call Dr. Adeline. Dr. Adeline told the analyst to give her address to Victor. Victor called her and made an appointment.

A week later Dr. Adeline was sitting behind her desk waiting for Victor in the room where she had her psychoanalytic couch. Her office was located on the fifth floor of a six-storey building in a residential district at the outskirts of the city. In the same building another psychoanalyst had an office, and other spaces were occupied by other businesses. Dr. Adeline's patients could park their cars next to the building and then either take an elevator or walk up to her office. During Dr. Adeline's working hours the office door was usually kept unlocked and a patient could just open it and walk into a comfortable waiting room furnished with armchairs. Behind one door in the waiting room there was a toilet and a kitchenette and behind a second door another comfortable room where Dr. Adeline conducted psychoanalysis. Through a large window in front of her couch one could see trees below in a public garden. Dr. Adeline's comfortable psychoanalytic chair was placed behind the couch. Her bookshelf, desk, and desk chair stood in front of the wall opposite the wall beside her couch. There was a big colourful rug on the floor. She had no secretary. Usually there would be a ten-minute break between her appointments, and after starting their work with Dr. Adeline, her analysands soon learned to come to their sessions just before their starting time. This way there would usually be no one waiting long in the waiting room. In expectation of Victor's first visit, that day Dr. Adeline kept both her office and therapy room doors open.

A tall, blond man who appeared to be in his early thirties, dressed in business suit and carrying a leather briefcase suddenly entered the waiting room and walked directly to the therapy room. With a big smile on his face, he said, "In order for you to know who I am" and put a personal business card on Dr. Adeline's desk. She was surprised. What she saw on the business card, written in big letters, was not Victor's name. For a moment she thought that this man was an intruder, perhaps a salesman, but before she could ask him to leave her office, since she was expecting someone else, the handsome man introduced himself verbally as Victor. Only then did Dr. Adeline notice Victor's name on the card, written in small letters underneath another name written in large ones, as if his own identity was hidden in the shadow of another person. Apparently the name written in big letters belonged to Victor's boss. This strange business card stayed in Dr. Adeline's mind. Only much later could she understand the card's symbolism.

Victor reported that at his university he had started to take classes in anthropology, changed his mind, and then studied business. When he came to see Dr. Adeline he was working for a well-known finance company, consulting with businesses, industries, as well as individuals, offering information and guidance about investments, loans, buying and selling stocks and bonds. The referring psychoanalyst's niece, Mariel, came from a rich family. A year earlier her father had been in a car accident that left him bedridden with a broken leg. He had also suffered from a brain injury and could not manage the family's finances. Because of this, the finance company where Victor worked was hired to help them. In fact Victor had met Mariel while working hard to put her family's finances in order.

In Dr. Adeline's presence, without showing any worry and continually smiling as if he were there to discuss a business venture, Victor insisted that he was a happy man for twenty hours each day, but apparently between two and six in the morning he was in another world. He had no name for his symptom. He did not have clear memories of being in a strange state of mind, although he was aware that it happened repeatedly. He could recall his heart beating very fast or finding himself in the bathroom without knowing when he had come there. There had been other girlfriends before Mariel, and they also had informed him of his waking up after midnight and behaving as if his and the girl friends' lives were in danger. These previous girlfriends had left him because of this symptom. When I heard this I wondered if Mariel was staying with him because he had rescued her family's finances.

Victor reported that he was fascinated with a tattoo on Mariel's left shoulder. For him, the tattoo looked like clouds of different colours. He could not come up with an explanation for why Mariel's tattoo commanded his interest. Meaningful associations about the tattoo would come later.

As a child Victor lived with his parents, a younger brother, and his maternal grandmother in a huge house overlooking a lake. His maternal grandfather died before Victor was born, and the house belonged to his maternal grandmother. Dr. Adeline realised that the lake Victor was referring to was the same lake bordering the town and the castle that she and I had visited years before. She knew that many rich families lived there.

Dr. Adeline met with Victor face to face three more times before agreeing to treat him. Victor came for treatment on his psychoanalyst's couch three times a week. During the face-to-face meetings and initial months of Victor's analysis Dr. Adeline collected data about his life and childhood events. The rest of this chapter is a summary of what she learned. My aim here is to introduce the reader to people who were important individuals in little Victor's life and to describe aspects of his developmental years. Obviously, in the following chapters we will learn more details about these individuals as well as other persons and events in this analysand's childhood.

Victor's mother was a housewife, but very busy with activities in several societal organisations. She had been married before, but her first husband had died when he slipped and fell from a ladder while fixing the roof of their house. Victor was nine months old when his mother became pregnant again. On many occasions his mother told him that when the newborn baby Richard was brought home from the hospital, Victor had demanded she "take him away". Little Victor had the impression that something had happened to his mother during her pregnancy and that his brother had been born "unhealthy". He did not know what was wrong with the pregnant mother and could not give details, but vaguely recalled that the family expected Richard to be epileptic, although adult Victor had no memory of his brother having had a seizure. From his early childhood on he perceived how the adult members of his family, especially his mother, continued to feel that Richard's life was in danger and that he had to be protected or he might die at any time. This meant that less attention was paid to little Victor's wishes and needs. For example, when the two boys were given tricycles in two different colours Richard demanded that, since Victor's tricycle was better, he wanted it himself. In order not to hurt little Richard the family made sure that the two boys exchanged their tricycles.

According to Victor, his mother did not exhibit usual loving and caring attitudes, nor did she speak of being proud of her children. She mostly behaved as if the children, especially Richard, should be hidden from others and be protected. Looking back, Victor also wondered why his mother was not aware of some *real* dangers. They were living in a house built on a hill. One side of the house had a view of the lake, and a sharply declining yard separated the other side of the house from a very busy street. A fence with a big iron gate stood between the yard and the street. The two little boys were allowed to go down the hill towards the gate on their tricycles. Now, adult Victor wondered what would have happened to him or Richard if their tricycles had hit the iron gate.

If the gate had been open they would have been killed due to the heavy traffic in the street. He now realised that his mother denied certain facts when the boys were growing up. The mother also behaved as if no noise was coming from the street below, no trucks were passing by, and only talked about the property's beautiful sunny view.

When Victor was born his father was the chief administrator of a very prestigious college and a well-known person in the small town where the family lived. Mostly wealthy people's children attended this college. While he was growing up Victor heard stories from his mother and maternal grandmother about his father experiencing anxiety attacks two months after Victor's birth. Apparently his father would feel that the earth was shaking and the floor under him might collapse. Victor was told how the family tried very hard to hide his father's anxiety episodes because it would have been shameful to people in the community and they did not want them to know what he was experiencing. In public he needed to behave as a prominent person should. Of course, Victor had no memories of his father's problems, which took place during the son's infancy. Victor recalled the father of his childhood as an easygoing person who, on and off, would still have brief "panic attacks". His father would sometimes appear very nervous, quickly pick up his keys, and then "disappear" from home as if there were an emergency. Little Victor would imagine that his father had gone to his office at the college. When the father returned home from a disappearance he would once more sit around in a leisurely manner. When Victor grew older and became a prepubertal child, his father no longer had such symptoms. Victor did not recall receiving open gestures of love or playfulness from the older man; his father's attitude towards him was similar to that of Victor's mother. Only after Victor was grown up enough to play tennis did he observe his father's strong competitive spirit. Watching his son play, Victor's father wanted him to not just win the match, but be as "in a war and kill his competitor".

Victor's parents were absent from the house most of the time, and his maternal grandmother looked after little Richard and Victor. Victor recalled how his mother referred to his grandmother's cooking as fattening and "unhealthy", but he could not recall if he hated or loved his grandmother's meals. Sometimes when his parents were away his grandmother would repaint furniture in new colours. It sounded like the older woman wanted some change in this house and she could attempt to do so only when her daughter and son-in-law were away from home; it was as if she needed a change from a house that had been the same for decades. As Victor was growing up he became aware of his parents' fear that when the grandmother died the mother's two sisters and one brother would fight over the house. They worried that the house would then be sold in order for all the siblings to get their share of the money. So, as a child, Victor developed a habit; he would go to his grandmother's room daily to check to see if she was still alive. It seemed that in the house Victor grew up in there was an atmosphere of expecting somebody's death—Richard's or grandmother's or even his own. The maternal grandmother did pass away when Victor was a university student studying anthropology. Belying their expectations, the mother's siblings caused no trouble and his parents continued to live in Victor's maternal grandmother's house.

Victor's paternal grandmother died when Victor was two months old. When he reported this to Dr. Adeline the patient added that he thought that his father's symptoms of the earth shaking and the floor collapsing might have something to do with his father's mother's illness and death. After all, Victor had been told that his father developed his symptoms when his son was two months old. The paternal grandmother had moved to this town from Berlin with her little boy in the midst of World War II, into a house not far from the maternal grandmother's house. Victor's paternal grandfather was killed at the Eastern front where Germans were fighting the Soviets when Victor's father was seven years old. Victor's father lived with his widowed mother until he was thirty-five years old, at which time he married and moved into his mother-in-law's house.

Victor said that his paternal grandfather had been a high-level SS officer. While Victor was growing up, adults in his family told him that his paternal grandfather managed to have himself transferred to the Eastern war zone and, in a sense, he had "committed suicide" by exposing himself to enemy fire because he had unknowingly participated in doing "bad things" while he was an SS officer. Victor had no idea what the "bad things" had been. There were no other references to his grandfather in the family while he was growing up, but he was given an image of him as a good man, a "martyr". This was all adult Victor knew about his paternal grandfather's life, and he never seemed to be preoccupied with thoughts about this ancestor whom he had never met.

In time we gradually learned more about events in Victor's life: he was told that he had vomiting spells over a period of two months when he was three years old and apparently was hospitalised. Six months or a year later he was hospitalised again, this time for a tonsillectomy. Apparently a nurse held him down while a surgeon tried to put a mask on his face to give him laughing gas, nitrous oxide. Little Victor fought against being "gassed". During surgery the anesthesia failed and he regained consciousness. Adult Victor could only recall seeing red forms, like clouds, moving around. One of his earliest memories is being at home after his tonsillectomy. Apparently he started screaming while he slept, but, he was told, would not wake up. His grandmother slapped his face hard to waken him, and he remembered opening his eyes and seeing his grandmother's "ugly face". He was horrified. Later he would have nightmares. Adult Victor did not recall the contents of his nightmares, but he did recall seeing frightening images resembling colourful "clouds" before falling asleep. When she heard about little Victor seeing colourful clouds during his tonsillectomy and later in his childhood before falling asleep, Dr. Adeline thought that Victor's interest in his girlfriend's tattoo was connected with his childhood experiences. Later in his analysis Victor, too, would reach the same conclusion and give further associations to the cloud images.

Victor had a more detailed description of another surgery—his circumcision at the age of eleven. It, also, was very traumatic. A mean-faced nurse, her hair under a head cover, held him tight to an operating table so that a mask could be put on his face to give him anesthetic and put him to sleep for surgery. Victor said: "I was panicked that I was going to be gassed. I did not want to be gassed". In his mind the memory of the mean-faced nurse was connected with the "ugly" face of his maternal grandmother who slapped his face to stop his screaming while he was sleeping.

It was unusual for boys in his town, and, as a matter of fact, in Germany, to be circumcised. However, Victor recalled his mother telling him that half of males on earth are circumcised. He did have a reason for this surgery, and it was connected to his experience as a Protestant living in a town where the majority of the population was Catholic. At home he heard remarks that Protestants were intelligent and sophisticated people and Catholics were not, and he developed a secret feeling that he was a "superior being", much better than the Catholic youngsters at his school who he felt should be "devalued". He had fights with the Catholic boys in his class, during which he was kicked on his penis and testicles. These encounters left scars on the skin covering his glans penis that made it painful for him to pull the foreskin back and clean it. Later he had difficulty urinating. This was why he had to be circumcised. After this event he was afraid of needles and doctors.

During his adolescence Victor began screaming at night. He could not recall what would initiate his screaming, but he remembered his mother telling him at breakfast, "You had another unquiet night". No one in the family seemed to be interested in finding out why Victor was screaming, and his condition became an accepted fact. During the daytime his parents, grandmother, and Victor lived a "normal life". While telling this story Victor stated that his screaming at night during adolescence was "nothing". From the very first meeting with this handsome blond man Dr. Adeline sensed that Victor was minimising and denying troublesome things about himself, as if they were happening in another world and to someone else.

Before proceeding further I wish to inform the reader that Victor gave the brief information about his SS officer paternal grandfather on the first day he met Dr. Adeline. The reader will note that the mental representation of this grandfather will not appear in Victor's treatment process until his third year on the couch. I will also examine psychological factors causing this long "silence".

CHAPTER THREE

A look at narcissism, splitting, depositing, dissociation, and encapsulation

When Dr. Adeline began consulting with me she told me how Victor would come to his sessions regularly, always smiling. He would talk non-stop, *analyse himself*, and behave as if he were the "best analysand" in the whole world. He reported daydreams in which he was being watched by a crowd of people in tribunes and applauded as the winner of a race at the Olympics. Victor would say how psychoanalysis was making him happy and how Dr. Adeline was the "best analyst" he could ever find. He behaved and talked as if he was forcing Dr. Adeline to adore him as her "best patient".

Victor was still living with his parents, just as his father had lived with his widowed mother until age thirty-five. Except for a few years when he attended a university in another town, he had never left his parental home. In a sense he was identifying with his father and most likely exhibiting some "separation-individuation problems" (Mahler, 1968). His mother washed his dirty clothes and ironed his shirts and trousers, he believed, in the "best possible way" a person could perform this function. After his treatment started he left his parents' home and, together with Mariel, found an apartment in the city where his analyst's office was located, next door to a building that belonged to the city's Psychoanalytic Society. Without saying it in words, he was implying by his action that he belonged to this society. He and Mariel had their own bedrooms, separated by a door. It was while living in this apartment that Victor recognised that Mariel suffered from colitis.

He continued taking his dirty laundry to his mother, as if he was entitled to wear clothes that were pressed "perfectly". After a while he stopped doing this, bought a washing machine, and took care of his own laundry. He implied that he had found his "independence" and was "getting well" quickly. All this time, during his sessions Victor did not dwell on his bizarre symptom of waking up after midnight and spending the next few hours in a different state of mind. Meanwhile, health insurance was paying for his psychoanalytic sessions. Dr. Adeline felt frustrated for being placed as if as part of a tribune watching Victor. This was her reason for consulting with me.

Let me first share with the reader what came to my mind when I listened to Dr. Adeline's reason for consulting with me: I worked with several analysands who lived under what I named as "glass bubbles" (Volkan, 1973, 1979, 1982, 2008; Volkan & Ast, 1992, 1994) and kept me outside of their lonely kingdoms as a spectator. Individuals with obvious and easily observable glass bubbles have narcissistic personality organisation. Persons with typical narcissistic personality organisation behave overtly as "Number One" in power or beauty or intelligence or in all these and related areas, and exhibit what became known in the psychoanalytic literature as a "grandiose self". After Heinz Kohut (1966, 1971) coined this term, Otto Kernberg (1970, 1975) who, unlike Kohut, dwelt on the object-relations conflicts of such individuals, made this term popular in describing the omnipotent part of the self that such patients exhibit overtly. Kernberg describes how a grandiose self is formed from the fusion of three elements: the real self, the ideal self, and the ideal object. The real self is the specialness of the child reinforced by early experiences with mother and other important persons with mothering functions in the child's environment. The ideal self is the self-image that is endowed with power, beauty, or wealth to compensate the child's normative frustration in his environment; the ideal self-image also helps the child manage disconcerting and difficult early emotions such as rage and envy. The ideal object is the fantasised image of the limitlessly providing mother. Individuals with typical narcissistic personality organisation often are seductive and strikingly articulate (Akhtar & Thomson, 1982) and use language in an autocentric manner for regulating self-esteem while exhibiting cognitive and emotional limitations (Bach, 2006; Volkan, 2010). Apparently Victor on the couch presented such characteristics. Such persons also possess covertly what I call a "hungry self", which consists of degraded and unwanted internalised self- and object images. They split off their hungry self from their grandiose self. The hungry self is usually externalised into the Other.

There are various types of narcissistic personality organisation, ranging from being "successful" to being "malignant". Successful ones achieve a position in life where their inner sense of exaggerated self-love, being "number one" and above others, is actually verified by hundreds, thousands, or millions of people when they become adored popular icons, leaders of organisations, or influential political figures. Such individuals, who possess intelligence, unconscious fantasies of being "saviours", and are capable of certain sublimations, achieve and maintain a "fit" between their psychological entitlement for greatness, adoration and the responses they receive from the external world. On the other end of the spectrum, there are persons who are impelled to experience "repeated aggressive triumphs" (Volkan & Ast, 1994) over others who represent the "hungry" aspects of their self-representations and threatening devalued object images, in order to feel unique, strong, entitled, and defensively omnipotent. Their narcissism is contaminated with paranoid expectations (Kernberg, 1975; Stone, 1989). There are even those who hide their grandiosity behind masochism (Cooper, 1989; Volkan, 2010). Listening to Dr. Adeline, I noted that Victor was behaving as if he possessed a "successful" narcissistic personality, but I heard no stories to suggest that, in his daily life, he had achieved such a status. While Victor talked about his family in his sessions with Dr. Adeline, his perception of his brother Richard as someone in need of protection was not degrading his brother. I noted no references to Victor collecting "aggressive triumphs". If he were involved in such activities during the early hours of the morning when he was in another world, he could not remember them. In any case, individuals with true "successful" or "malignant" narcissistic personality organisations usually would not seek therapeutic help.

Patients with any type of narcissistic personality organisation develop expected transference manifestations as soon as they start their psychoanalysis: sometimes the analysand is "great", and the analyst is "bad", as they respectively represent the patient's grandiose self and hungry self. Sometimes both the patient and the analyst are "superior beings" and someone outside of the analyst's office "stinks". Even when the patient feels that both he and the analyst are "Number One", he has a need to protect the grandiose self. The patient makes the analyst "Number One" only in order to be adored by a superior other. The analyst can observe grandiose expressions in the patient's words and behaviour, but she is not allowed to become a genuine partner in exploring the meaning of such expressions; the patient, alone by himself, may be "curious" about what he is saying or doing and come up with his own explanations of his behaviour patterns. What I heard from Dr. Adeline was that Victor related to her as would a person with a narcissistic personality.

I agree with Arnold Modell (1975) that the mental trauma inflicted when a child is building his or her sense of identity—that is, a subjective sense of reliable and permanent sameness (Erikson, 1956)—may lead to the establishment of a precocious and vulnerable sense of autonomy supported by fantasies of omnipotence. Modell states that, by doing so, vulnerable children may also attempt to defend themselves against excessive maternal intrusiveness. It was clear that during his developmental years Victor experienced two surgeries and mental trauma. In his childhood history "maternal intrusiveness" needed to be explored later. I must add that identity problems and problems in the distribution of narcissism are always related. We expect to find problems with the distribution of love of self as well as love of others (objects) when the identity is not cohesive. This way the child may develop the nucleus of a grandiose self as well as the beginning of a hungry self and keep the two parts split off from one another.

Developmentally, until a small child begins to tolerate and maintain ambivalence, there is a "normal" developmental splitting of opposing images. As researcher Daniel Stern (1985) noted, an infant is fed four to six times a day and each feeding experience produces different degrees of pleasure. Stern illustrates that as the child grows up, different experiences become categorised in the child's mind as "good" and "bad". If the child cannot fully accomplish the integrative task, due to biological as well as environmental reasons, the individual's identity, even in adulthood, remains divided. For persons such as those with borderline personality organisation as well as narcissistic personality organisation, the normal *developmental* splitting evolves as a *defensive* splitting. In other words, as they grow up, such individuals continue to maintain two unintegrated parts, to one degree or another. Towards the end of the first year of life or during the second, a child may put down a foundation for the future typical narcissistic personality organisation.

I have studied the family stories of patients with narcissistic personality organisation (Volkan, 2010; Volkan & Ast, 1992, 1994). Although the mother (or a mothering person) of such a patient was cold and ungiving, she saw the child as someone "special", perhaps more beautiful than other siblings or a "saviour of the family name". One Catholic mother prone to depression, in search of an idealised father of her own, viewed her son as special and had daydreams of his growing up to be the Pope (idealised father). Her perception of her child as unique was, if you will, "pushed into" the developing identity of the infant through the mother-child interaction. For example, while her son was growing up she gave him daily enemas. This way the boy would always be "clean" and suitable for her image of a future Pope. Victor sometimes would refer to his mother as "lion mother", determined to protect her children, especially Richard. She also made Victor a special child, a protector of his younger brother and the family. But, she was not a "regular" loving mother. She was a "distant" one. More details about little Victor's view of himself as a "saviour" will be noted in the following chapters. Victor's description of his mother's lack of recognition of certain real dangers for her small children while they were riding their tricycles might have also played a role in inhibiting Victor's integrative ego capacity.

Let me briefly mention another factor associated with family members that may play a significant role in laying down the foundation for a future narcissistic personality organisation in a child: a mother or a caretaker who has a well formed mental representation of a dead child or a dead adult may deposit this mental representation into the living child, thus making the child's self-representation a special container. If what is deposited into the child's developing self-representation is a grand image, it may function as an initiator for a future grandiose self.

"Depositing" (Volkan, 1987, 2010, 2014c, 2015; Volkan, Ast, & Greer, 2002) is closely related to "identification", but it is in some ways significantly different. Identification, a common concept in psychoanalysis, refers to a person's unconscious introjection and assimilation of another person's realistic as well as fantasised self-images—and ego and superego functions associated with them—through actual interactions and even imagined interactions with that other person. Sometimes patients refer to incorporative fantasies, such as imagining eating the object, when they refer to their attempts at identification. Let me now focus on identifications in childhood, which provide building blocks for a personality organisation. True identification is only possible after children separate their self-representations from the representations of others. In identification, the child is the primary active partner. In depositing, the adult person is the active partner who plants his specific images into the developing self-representation of the child. In other words, the adult person uses the child (mostly unconsciously) as a permanent reservoir for certain self- and other images belonging to that adult and initiates the child's certain psychological tasks linked to these transferred images. The experiences that created these mental images in the adult are not accessible to the child. Yet, those mental images are pushed into the child without the experiential/contextual framework that created them. Melanie Klein's (1946) "projective identification" can explain such a process. However, I wish to use the term "depositing" to illustrate how parenting individuals create a psychological DNA in the child.

Consider for instance, the situation of the "replacement child" (Ainslie & Solyom, 1986; Cain & Cain, 1964; Green & Solnit, 1964; Legg & Sherick, 1976; Poznanski, 1972; Volkan & Ast, 1997). Parents (or parenting individuals) have a mental representation of their deceased child or a lost important adult. When a new child comes along after the parents experience a loss, the child, of course, has no actual experience with the dead sibling or lost adult. Mother or other mothering persons "deposit" their own internalised self-representation of the dead or lost person—with associated tasks—into the developing self-representation of the newborn child, creating a "psychological gene". One mother enduring complicated mourning viewed her young child as a link to dead siblings, thus the child was perceived as "immortal" and omnipotent. Although her complicated mourning process made her cold and psychologically ungiving as a mother, she engaged in a relationship with the child, a relationship defined by an intense pressure on the child to attend and respond to her mother's own psychological needs. What was "deposited" into Victor's developing self-representation by his parents will be the main topic of this book.

Because patients with narcissistic personality organisation need to protect their grandiose selves, Arnold Modell (1975) referred to the initial phase of the analysis of such individuals as the "cocoon phase", as these patients hide their grandiose selves as if in a cocoon. I suggest that the analogy of a "glass bubble" is more useful because it describes a transparent enclosure that permits its occupant to assess the world outside without being encroached upon and thus it enhances the patients' sense of omnipotence and self-sufficiency. Typical patients with narcissistic personality organisation, while absorbed with self-interest, do have *intense* relationships with others; they watch people through the metaphorical glass, in a sense, to see if others are going to adore or devalue them. Such patients will react to others according to their conscious and unconscious assessments of them, and they want to know if there are dangerous objects out there that may disturb their lonely kingdoms. Some of them actually speak about how they feel themselves behind a glass while interacting with the analyst or another important person. Or the analyst may feel that her words hit a transparent enclosure surrounding a patient and boomerang back to her. While Victor was "forcing" his analyst to remain a spectator, he would never miss his sessions with her, and this reflected his intense relationship, under his control, with Dr. Adeline.

Listening to Dr. Adeline, I pictured Victor under a metaphorical glass bubble while lying on his analyst's couch. But I also noticed that his case did not fully fit the definition of a narcissistic personality organisation. A person with narcissistic personality organisation uses splitting of self- and object images as a main mental defence and covertly is aware of the existence of his or her "hungry self". One of my patients with a narcissistic personality was a handsome and articulate medical student. He kept at least one hundred cans of food in his kitchen. If their number diminished he would sense his "hungry self", rush to a grocery store, and buy more canned food. Such an individual usually externalises her hungry self into the Other in order to keep her grandiose self from being contaminated with unwanted elements. But, external circumstances, such as being fired from a job or even having a pimple on her face brings the "hungry self" to the individual's attention. Under such a circumstance this individual may even feel depressed and this becomes her reason for seeking psychoanalysis. When she faces humiliation or rejection, such an individual may also feel obliged do something dramatic that would keep her superiority alive. In my book *Animal Killer* (Volkan, 2014c) I described how a male patient with narcissistic personality organisation, in this case a rather malignant one, would fly over a herd of deer and machine gun them after experiencing rejection or humiliation.

Victor, the happiest man on earth for twenty hours each day and the "best analysand" who was analysing himself on an analyst's couch was, for up to four hours after midnight, in another world, apparently a dangerous one. But, he *did not* know who he was and with what internalised or externalised object images he was dealing while in this other world. Victor's main defence mechanism was dissociation, which had created a dissociated self with its own corresponding object images and affects. Furthermore, he erected a border for this dissociative self and "encapsulated" it (Rosenfeld, 1965; Rosenfeld, 1992). Victor learned the existence of his dissociated self mainly because others who observed it described it to him. Also Victor witnessed things, such as his bed mattress out of place or "waking up" in the bathroom, that lead to his assumption that he was involved in activities he could not remember later. Amnesia was present in his condition.

Nevertheless, there is confusion in the psychoanalytic literature about the term "dissociation" and separating it from the term "splitting". Salman Akhtar (2009) reminded us that Donald Winnicott (1960) had used "splitting" and "dissociation" almost synonymously. Akhtar stated: "… it should be noted that, over the years, these terms acquired a diagnostic 'buzz-word' significance; 'dissociation' is linked with multiple personality or 'dissociative character' and … 'splitting' with borderline conditions" (p. 82) and, I must add, with narcissistic personality organisation. Ira Brenner (1994, 2001, 2004, 2014) contributed greatly to our understanding of dissociation. Brenner described dissociation "as a defense against anxiety in the here and now through the reactivation of altered states associated with earlier trauma" (Brenner, 2004, p. 11). Elsewhere he wrote:

> Under traumatic conditions in childhood, one's mind might not be able to reconcile the contradictions necessary for psychic and, possibly, physical survival. For example, in order to maintain an attachment to a murderous, sexually violating mother, there might be a coalescing of self- and object representations into seemingly separate selves maintained in hypnotic states. (Brenner, 2014, p. 56)

Brenner was aware that dissociation "may change in its function and be employed later on a defense against the perceived internal danger of intolerable affects and instinctual strivings" (Brenner, 1994, p. 481). He described a hierarchical continuum of dissociative personality pathology. For example, he linked dissociation to puzzling sleepy trans-like states, minor lapses of attention, or brief memory loss. But, he also described persons with multiple personality organisation who utilise dissociation all the time. I suggested that individuals who have multiple personality organisation exhibit an *advanced* version of low-level (psychotic) personality organisation (Volkan, 2015). The internal world of people with the latter organisation contains fragmented self- and object images with their associated affects. If the fragmented self-images and corresponding object images evolve to possess distinct characteristics and become stable enough for the individual to sense them, as if various identities (personalities) exist within the individual, we say that this person has multiple personality organisation (Abse, 1983; Brenner, 1994, 2001, 2004, 2014; Kluft, 1993). The person may give her different identities names— one is Madeline, the other one Grace and still another one Fatima. One of these personalities, if advanced enough, will not recognise the lower-level ones since the function of repression is available to it. But this does not mean that the advanced personality will not sense the co-existence of the other personality or personalities in one way or another. The lower-level personalities, without the benefit of repression, may be aware of the existence of the highest one and each other. Ira Brenner has seen very destructive, primitive, aggressively based selves not know about the others. Here, there may be an omnipotent, destructively grandiose flavour to the dissociative barrier between selves. Such a self may violently reject the notion of others, especially weak, needy selves; or if she is aware or becomes aware of the others, she may also want to kill them off and take over exclusive control of the body (Brenner, 2015).

We can imagine Victor as someone with two personalities. The happy Victor on Dr. Adeline's couch did not know if the other Victor who was described to him by others had another name or if the second one knew the existence of the first one. An analyst can observe clearly how a patient with narcissistic personality organisation externalises his hungry self into the Other. In Victor's situation there was no need to externalise a dissociated self since it was firmly encapsulated (Rosenfeld, 1992; Rosenfeld, 1965) and was subjected to amnesia. During his psychoanalytic sessions Victor would talk about his brother who was perceived as "defective" by the family. But it was difficult to think that he was externalising his encapsulated self into Richard. In fact, Victor did not know if his encapsulated dissociated self was a degraded one or not. He was told by his different girlfriends that it was a self who was in a dangerous environment, but not a degraded one. This self was also ready to escape from danger or fight against the dangerous Other. So far, Dr. Adeline, too, had not yet met the second Victor.

Everybody's unconscious is very adept at finding ways to make us sense things that are not in our awareness, at least in symbolic ways. Victor, who could not describe his dissociated and encapsulated self—and its related object images and affects—had an awareness of its symbolic representation. In another repeating daydream Victor leaves the Olympic arena and walks alone in the countryside. He has a big egg under his arm. The egg contains "catastrophes" or "chaos". Victor needs to stay absolutely quiet. If he makes any noise the eggshell may crack open and "catastrophes" or "chaos" will ooze out. While reporting this daydream Victor exhibited no anxiety. Instead he fantasised putting an extra shell, like shiny gift wrapping paper around the egg (encapsulation) to make sure that nothing escaped from it. Victor's repeating fantasy illustrated that he was carrying his dissociated self, which contained "catastrophes" or "chaos", under his arm. In another fantasy Victor came across a castle and realised that this castle belonged to his family. He also saw a knight on a white horse next to the castle. He was most astonished when, shortly after having this daydream image of the knight, he found a picture he had painted when he was a five-year-old that depicted a knight on a white horse. Dr. Adeline and I suspected that the knight on the horse stood for his grand self who might eliminate any "catastrophe" or "chaos" if it came out of the egg.

I learned that during his first year of treatment Victor added a bird to his repeating daydream of walking into the countryside after leaving the Olympic arena. A small bird landed on his shoulder and this made him "feel nice". Apparently, the patient had no curiosity about the little bird. Later, in a similar fantasy, the bird had more colours. Dr. Adeline thought that the bird represented Victor's transference image of his analyst. After all, she was sitting behind Victor, like the small bird sitting on her patient's shoulder, and the bird in the fantasy made Victor feel better. Sometime later the bird's face became like a lion's, recalling Victor's reference to his mother as a "lion mother". When Dr. Adeline shared what came to her mind with Victor he would not stay with this topic; he did not wish to hear that he might need someone else to make him feel "nice" or perceive someone as he had perceived his own childhood mother. In his consciousness, he only wanted to keep Dr. Adeline the "best analyst", but under his control, and to be adored by her. At this time he stopped reporting further associations, as well as daydreams, and returned to being a "super analysand". But, Dr. Adeline also noticed her patient making an appointment with a physician for a physical checkup in order to verify that he did not have skin cancer or another ailment. She also heard Victor's wish to finish his work with her because he had already become "well". Only when Dr. Adeline linked Victor's fascination with Mariel's tattoo, which looked like clouds, to his seeing cloud-shaped red images after his tonsillectomy did her patient seem to listen to her and accept what she had said.

Before reaching adolescence Victor felt like a "superior" being and devalued the Catholic students. This was his only clear story of having devalued images out there, and because of this he was punished. Having an encapsulated dissociated self was allowing him to remain "superior" without the memory of danger and punishment and without affects connected with such a "catastrophe". Sometimes Victor would say that fear of physicians might be a part of the "catastrophes" within the egg under his arm. By now, Dr. Adeline was aware that her attempts to explore, together with Victor, the genetic reasons for his symptom, such as the early traumas reported above, would frighten him. In any case, Victor would not take such a psychological journey at this time. She was also aware that she needed to expand the above formulation about understanding Victor's dissociated and encapsulated self and search for other factors to understand Victor's internal world better.

Victor's overt self-representation, and corresponding object images, such as the "best analyst", that supported it while he was on the analyst's couch, were linked with exaggerated narcissism. The analyst needed to tolerate and accept such a condition and keep her sense of frustration or boredom to herself. Exploring the nature of Victor's transference manifestations would quickly disturb the patient since his main concern was to protect his grandiosity and isolate and encapsulate his dissociated self. Tolerance of Victor's overt transference manifestations would be the best approach for a slow development of a therapeutic alliance and for Victor to slowly evolve a workable and stable transference relatedness that would correspond to the transference neurosis of a person with neurotic personality organisation. Then Victor would be ready to be curious, together with his analyst, about his internal world, and this development would be a tool for working through his psychological problems. I told Dr. Adeline that sometimes it takes many months, even years, for a patient such as Victor to arrive at this new phase. Dr. Adeline had similar thoughts, but having another analyst thinking the same way, I believe, was helpful for her.

Later in this book I will examine how adults deposited mental images into Victor's developing self-representation along with the transmission of trauma from one generation to those that follow. As Ira Brenner (2014) also observes, intergenerational transmission of trauma is a contributor to the creation of dissociative personality.

CHAPTER FOUR

The "Firefighter"

Listening to Dr. Adeline I noted—and she agreed—that her patient was treating Mariel and his former girlfriends in ways similar to how he was treating his analyst. There seemed to be no genuine, loving, sharing, or interactive relationship between him and his girlfriends. He bragged about his ability to keep his penile erection longer than any other man during intercourse before ejaculation. He connected this to his circumcision and talked about how his glans penis was directly touching his underwear. He believed that this was making his glans penis less sensitive so he could keep his erection longer than any other man. These were his intellectualised remarks. Victor's emphasis was his being in and winning the Olympic competition for sexual performance. He was a "superior" being.

Victor also exhibited an exaggerated narcissistic orientation at his workplace. He stated that he worked for the "best" finance company and, by sitting in front of a computer at work, as well as at home day and night and at weekends, he had found the "best" customers for the company. He gave the impression that he was the closest person to his boss in the whole world. However, in Dr. Adeline's mind there was confusion about what Victor's real position in this finance company was; she had learned that in reality he was not making much money.

On many occasions, while on the couch, Victor would talk about his activities between his psychoanalytic sessions. I imagined him relating these events as if he were reading a newspaper and reporting the latest news, especially those stories supporting his greatness. Sometimes he would tell childhood stories and refer to his fantasies because he knew that psychoanalysts were interested in such things. As time passed, his analyst learned that her talkative patient kept some of his activities secret. For example, it would take a long time for Dr. Adeline to hear that Victor and Mariel had moved from their apartment next to the Psychoanalytic Society building in the city to live in her mother's home. Later he and Mariel would move out and share a place, also in the same town. During the evenings Mariel would leave him before the appearance of his expected dissociate self and sleep in a different room or return to her mother's house. Victor would not examine why he kept some of his activities secret. I thought that because, some months after starting his psychoanalysis, he had left his parents' house and moved to the city as "proof' of his achieving independence, he did not wish to show his analyst that he had lost this "proof".

In the previous chapter I reported that Dr. Adeline told Victor about the possible connection between Mariel's tattoo that looked like clouds and Victor's childhood perceptions of "clouds" following his tonsillectomy. She was linking Victor's observation of something in the external world with an event that was a production of Victor's internal world. Mariel's tattoo was a reality in the external world, and seeing images of colourful clouds was a product of Victor's internal world. What Dr. Adeline had done can be explained by a concept that Peter Giovacchini (1969, 1972) named "linking interpretations". Later, I expanded the application of linking interpretations and illustrated them with several clinical examples (Volkan, 1976, 1987, 2010, 2015). Giovacchini based his description of linking interpretation on Freud's (1900) concept of day residue in dreams. As day residue, insignificant impressions derived from the real world—seeing a police car chasing a speeding vehicle on the motorway or passing a billboard depicting a smiling woman holding a milk bottle—join infantile aggressive or sexual wishes to initiate the content of dreams. Giovacchini applied Freud's understanding of day residue to the clinical setting, stating, "An interpretation may make a casual connection by referring to the day residue which may be the stimulus for the flow of the patient's associations or for some otherwise unexplainable behavior" (Giovacchini, 1969, p. 180). Giovacchini and I first noted the usefulness of linking interpretations at the first phase of working with patients with poor reality testing, such as patients with borderline or psychotic personality organisation. Such interpretations link events in external reality to intrapsychic phenomena and promote contact with reality.

Earlier Rudolph Loewenstein (1951, 1958) described preparatory interpretations during the beginning phase of a neurotic person's analysis. Preparatory interpretations primarily focus on how something in a patient's internal world stimulates expected behaviour in certain circumstances. The analyst names the internal phenomenon without an in-depth description of what might have caused it. For example, the analyst notes that a male patient consistently tries to avoid competition. The analyst then suggests that the patient is bound in some kind of unconscious rivalry as demonstrated by his avoidance of competition. By stating that the patient's external behaviour is due to an internal motive, the therapist awakens the patient's curiosity about his internal world and helps him to explore his unconscious rivalry. If the patient who avoids competition joins the analyst he may begin to notice certain aspects of his oedipal issues.

In making a preparatory interpretation the analyst names an internal phenomenon that he knows exists in human psychology. Then he refers to an external event as the manifestation of this internal phenomenon. It is as if preparatory interpretations reflect the internal's effect on the external, whereas linking interpretations demonstrate the effect of the external on the internal. Clearly, both linking and preparatory "interpretations" are incomplete. Only over time will they encompass ever-widening material.

I noted that Dr. Adeline was making "linking interpretations" and I was in favour of it. This, I thought, would indirectly encourage a patient such as Victor to follow what his analyst was doing and come up with other external and internal events that could be linked with one another. Making linking interpretations could initiate or solidify a working alliance between a patient such as Victor and his analyst without making the patient more defensive or anxious. I thought that, at this point, making preparatory interpretations would be a more difficult approach in helping Victor to become involved with his analyst and examine his internal world with her.

Dr. Adeline linked two events Victor was involved in to produce more information for understanding Victor's psychology and a hidden transference manifestation. The event connected with Victor's internal motivation was happening whenever Victor came to his psychoanalytic sessions. I learned that Dr. Adeline kept a small rug at the entrance to her therapy room. Victor had developed a habit; he would not only step on this little rug, but always try to smooth it out with one foot and arrange it to be as parallel as possible to the doorframe before entering the therapy room. His leg movement suggested he was ironing the rug. Obviously he had internal and unconscious motivations for developing this habit.

The external event was not a current one. Towards the end of the first year of his analysis Victor described the story of this external event that took place when he was eleven years old, most likely after his circumcision. A closer look would show the possibility that it might have happened due to an internal impulse when young Victor was in a dissociative state. However, Victor on the couch described it as an external event. During his childhood his parents traditionally lit a candle while sitting in the family room after dinner. Victor remembered one evening being on the second floor and seeing his parents coming up the stairs. He asked them: "Did you blow out the flame?" They answered "Yes". His mother told him to go to bed, since everything was alright. The next morning when the family members came down to the living room they found it filled with smoke. The candle from the night before had not been extinguished and had melted and fallen on the carpet, burning a portion of it. Apparently the fire extinguished itself; otherwise the whole family would have faced great danger to their lives.

When she first heard this story Dr. Adeline did not know if young Victor, in a dissociated state, started the fire himself after his parents and Richard went to their bedrooms and then put it out once he was no longer in his dissociated state. However, when he talked about the fire in the family room Victor presented it as an external event that had taken place outside his own involvement. What was crucial to the story was his parents' developing an idea that Victor possessed a sixth sense, since he had asked them to be sure the candle was out; for them young Victor was capable of foreseeing danger and saving himself and his family members from death. After this event his family called him "Firefighter" and perceived him as a genuine "disaster protector". To memorialise this event, his mother cut off part of the carpet that was not burned and dedicated it to Victor as a "gift". This piece of carpet was kept it in the attic for decades.

I knew how Victor's mother used to iron her son's clothes "perfectly". When I heard of his "ironing" his analyst's little carpet with his foot, the first thing that came to my mind was his trying to make Dr. Adeline's office a "perfect" location. After learning how Victor became the

"Firefighter" of his family just before he entered adolescence, I thought that his peculiar way of smoothing and moving the analyst's carpet at the therapy room door could have another meaning. It could be understood as putting a fire out and saving the analyst's life, and Victor as the analyst's saviour could be the unspoken transference. Expected deaths and needing a saviour were aspects of Victor's developmental years.

Dr. Adeline brought Victor's habit of adjusting the rug to his awareness and made a link between it and his being perceived, at age eleven, as a "disaster protector". She made no further transference references so as not to discourage Victor from opening up and providing more associations. If she focused too much on Victor's hidden feelings about her at this time, most likely he would perceive it as an intrusion into his defensive "self-analysis", his being the "best analysand", and his analyst being the "best analyst". Following Dr. Adeline's linking of the two events, Victor shared with Dr. Adeline how his becoming his brother Richard's saviour was firmly crystallised after he became the "disaster protector" for the family. Victor recalled how his parents told him openly: "*Passe auf Deinen Bruder auf!*" This meant that he should be careful with his brother, not hurt him, and take care of him. Victor realised that his parents had certain deficiencies; they were not able to take good care of Richard and therefore they obliged Victor to do it.

Victor moved on from his routine way of behaving on the analyst's couch and began genuinely wondering about his mother's and father's lives, moods, and behaviour patterns and allowing Dr. Adeline to join him in wondering about his environment during his developmental years. When Victor was a child at home there were no references to his mother's first husband who, it may be recalled, died after falling off a ladder. It was as if her life before she married Victor's father was a "secret" kept from her son. Who was her first husband? How did she feel when he died? Was she in mourning when she moved in with her mother and searched for a new husband? As for Victor's father, he had been living with his mother. We learned that his future wife perceived him as a "sissy", but married him nevertheless and took him from his mother's house to her mother's house. In spite of his being a highly educated man and having a prestigious job, it became clearer that Victor's father then "submitted" himself to a life in another house also dominated by an older woman, his mother-in-law. Victor thought that his father had no life of his own.

Listening to this information passed on to me by Dr. Adeline I thought it might be possible that Victor's mother had not fully mourned the death of her first husband when she married her second husband. It should be remembered that Victor's father had lost his mother when Victor was two months old. I imagined that complicated mourning of Victor's mother, joined with her husband's mourning, complicated Victor's separation-individuation issues. Victor himself was telling Dr. Adeline how his mother was a "lion mother", always worried about the health of her children from her second marriage and always concerned for their safety. But, for some reason that Dr. Adeline and I did not know yet, since his babyhood Victor's brother's image in the family had remained "unstable". According to the family perception, Richard was "breakable". From his early childhood on, Victor was given the task of being his "defective" brother's protector. After the fire incident, it appeared that Victor's task had become an accepted myth in the family history. Dr. Adeline knew that after starting his analysis her patient was calling his brother *daily*, checking on him, and continuing to function as the "Firefighter", a protector of the life of a "defective" brother. Richard was not as educated as his older brother, but had a steady job and girlfriend. Victor told Dr. Adeline that Richard was seeing a psychiatrist.

After Dr. Adeline brought his habit of symbolically putting a "fire" out before entering her therapy room to Victor's attention, he stopped his physical preoccupation with the analyst's little carpet. He "allowed" his analyst to become curious with him about the possibility of consequences of his parents' mourning and his mother's part in crystallising the "saviour" role for Victor in order to prevent further losses. Soon, however, Victor stopped being curious about his internal world and reverted to his usual way of relating to his analyst. In order to show the analyst that his recalling the memory from age eleven and talking about it had made him "well" quickly, he stopped calling his brother.

Interestingly, after losing Victor's unusual excessive interest in him, Richard abruptly gave up his work and his girlfriend, moved out of his apartment, and returned to his parents' home. In a sense, Dr. Adeline thought, Richard *became* a "defective" person, and his parents once more made him the centre of their rapt attention. It should be recalled that at this time Victor was no longer living at his parent's house. He was also in charge of his own dirty laundry. But he would, without Mariel, go to his parent's house for dinner almost every day. He began observing in an obsessive manner how his parents were looking after Richard as if he was "defective". For weeks, session after session, Victor did not speak about anything else but the perception of his brother as a defective person, his parents' anxiety about Richard's well-being, and their immersion in worries about Richard. In a sense, the situation that existed in Victor's childhood became reincarnated. This way, Dr. Adeline had a firsthand observation of Richard's early childhood environment. However, her patient had lost his curiosity; instead of wondering what had developed, now he was only verbalising a description of the new situation in the family. This development also was instrumental in cracking the encapsulation of his dissociative state and allowing Victor to remember, feel, and express aspects of his dissociate state without fully understanding it.

One day he entered the analyst's bathroom and when he looked at the mirror he saw a rat laughing madly. Immediately he thought, "Am I going mad?" and the image disappeared. He began presenting dreams to his analyst. In most of them he was in an enclosed (encapsulated) place. He dreamed of being in a dark location from which he could not get out because of an obstruction. This dream reminded him of being stuck in a dark attic for several hours when he was a child after another boy closed the hatch and left him there. In another dream he saw himself saying, "Let's get out now! Hurry!" Then he dreamt of being in his bedroom. He tried to open the door, but it started spinning around and around, becoming like a big boomerang coming back to hit him, and he could not get out. In still another dream there were two rooms, one big and the other small. Dr. Adeline thought that, most likely, two rooms represented his overt grandiose self and his dissociative self. He tried to put the two locations together to create a single place but he was unsuccessful. This last dream pointed to the aim of treatment of someone such as Victor whose self-representation is not integrated. Such patients require, borrowing a term from Melanie Klein (1946), "crucial juncture" experiences in order to integrate their split or fragmented self- and object images with their associated opposing affect derivatives. At this time Victor would not give useful associations and would not work on his dream images. He was not yet ready to have a "crucial juncture" experience. In order to have such an experience Victor first needed to know and sense what psychological issues, self- and object images, were hidden in his encapsulated dissociative state and also to identify with the analyst's reality testing, taming, and integrating functions.

For the first time Victor also told Dr. Adeline that once when he was in his twenties, in a dissociate state, he attacked his father, dislocating the older man's arm. On a different occasion, again in a dissociate state, he tried to strangle Richard. He would not recall actual actions, but he realised what he had done after coming out of his second world. There were aggressive aspects of Victor when he was in this second world. He presented no anxiety reporting these events and dreams and would not give workable associations to them.

Victor's remaining an obsessive observer of his brother's situation abruptly took a new turn when Richard informed his older brother that he had an impulse to kill people by pushing them in front of approaching trains in an underground subway. Richard was full of rage. He also told Victor that he wanted to murder his parents and himself. Victor gave the above information on the couch, also without exhibiting any emotion. Dr. Adeline thought that Richard was responding with rage to his return to his parental home and being treated as a "defective" person. One day Victor reported how Richard had a car accident, hitting a tree while trying to avoid an approaching vehicle. Once more Victor seemed not to be anxious as he reported his brother's accident. Instead Dr. Adeline felt anxious that Richard might actually be trying to commit suicide. She was facing an unusual situation. How would she feel if Richard actually killed himself or other persons? What was her responsibility as Victor's analyst in preventing a tragedy? She informed her patient that there was an urgent matter for them to discuss and told him that something had to be done about his brother's threats before she and Victor could continue their analytic work together. She urged Victor to inform his brother's psychiatrist and/or the police about what Richard had told him. Otherwise, she would be obliged legally to get in touch with appropriate authorities to stop the possibility of Richard killing innocent persons in the subway, his parents, or himself. Furthermore, the analyst stated that by demanding this she was also protecting the analytic work between her and Victor; if she became anxious she could not hold on to her psychoanalytic identity. She added that if Richard became a murderer or committed suicide Victor would have bad feelings and this itself would also interfere with their analytic work. When Dr. Adeline stopped talking apparently Victor said: "But if my parents are killed and my brother commits suicide I will need you more!" Nevertheless, Victor came to his next session and informed her that he had talked with his parents as well as Richard's psychiatrist about Richard. Apparently Richard's psychiatrist gave his patient medication and talked with him. Soon Richard calmed down and declared that he no longer had any intention of committing murder or suicide. Victor's analysis continued.

CHAPTER FIVE

A dead old man whose heart kept beating

Halfway through Victor's second year in psychoanalysis, I did not speak with Dr. Adeline for many months. When she got in touch with me again she informed me about the following events: one day on his analyst's couch, as if he was giving a weather report, Victor said: "By the way, yesterday Mariel and I got engaged!" Victor had not bothered to let his analyst know that he was going to be engaged. Dr. Adeline learned that many months before Victor and Mariel's engagement took place Mariel had gone to a tattoo parlour where flowers and leaves were added to her tattoo. This way her tattoo no longer looked like the scary "clouds" he used to fantasise after his tonsillectomy; now it appeared "friendly". Dr. Adeline thought that Mariel's tattoo was no longer a reminder of the egg, filled with "catastrophes". I do not know if Victor asked Mariel to do this or if, sensing his response to her tattoo, she volunteered to change the tattoo's appearance.

Dr. Adeline also learned that Mariel's father, still recovering from his car accident, had developed an infection and his health had worsened. It appeared that the idea of Mariel's father approaching death was a factor in Victor's decision to become engaged to her even though he did not have enough money to buy a "superior" engagement ring. A day after her engagement, without Victor, Mariel went on vacation to Portugal. It was difficult for me to understand this couple's relationship. While she was away Mariel's father died and she returned and attended the funeral with Victor. Victor became the "Man", the "Saviour", and the "Firefighter" of Mariel's family.

Victor moved to a farmhouse that belonged to his fiancée's family and then rented an apartment on the third floor of a big building and bragged about this building having six bathrooms. Apparently he let his analyst know about moving to this new place some months after this change had taken place. The story and the psychological importance of this "big building" would become clear much later, as we shall see. On and off Victor provided important data and allowed himself to be curious about their deeper meanings, but basically he was still keeping Dr. Adeline as a spectator. At this time the story and psychological significance of this building with six bathrooms, and especially its third floor, were Victor's "secrets". Dr. Adeline did know that Mariel would not sleep with him all night and that she had her own bedroom in this apartment.

Dr. Adeline learned much more about Mariel's physical health. She was suffering from ulcerative colitis, abdominal cramps, diarrhea, and rectal bleeding. This made her a "defective" individual. Dr. Adeline noted that Victor's obsession with defective Richard was condensed with her patient finding another "defective" person to save. Richard, who had apparently calmed down, was on medication, and working well with his psychiatrist, was no longer a good target for Victor's need to rescue. Instead Victor thought that Mariel's ulcerative colitis was getting worse because she had been worrying about his nightly symptoms. In a sense, Victor once more created his childhood environment in his present life: there was a death—this time Mariel's father— and a defective individual—this time Mariel, and a "saviour"—again Victor. Instead of developing such a story within the transference and putting it into words, Victor created and found a scenario in which his childhood environment once more came to life through actions. His new idea and belief in "getting well" and being "healthy" evolved as did his wish to soon marry Mariel. When wedding plans were made Victor checked his mother's list of people she was planning to invite to her son's wedding, found some of them "unwanted", and asked his mother to delete them from her list. He and Mariel got married one year after their engagement. One and a half years later Mariel became pregnant. Her pregnancy would be a complicated one, and her diarrhea and rectal bleeding symptoms would flare up periodically. There was even talk of her having an abortion.

Before his engagement Victor spent many hours a day protecting Mariel's family's finances. Apparently Mariel's mother was not going along with some of his suggestions. But, since Victor was not telling details, Dr. Adeline could not fully understand what her patient was actually doing. She heard that his involvement with Mariel's family financial affairs was interfering with his work at the finance company; he even said that his position at the company was now in danger. Victor was having thoughts of quitting the company, finding his own clients, and working for himself. Much later Victor would tell his analyst that, at this time, he was becoming aware that the "best boss" anyone could have was stealing his clients' money.

While these changes were taking place in Victor's life, Dr. Adeline did not communicate with me. Then I received an email from her. She wrote: "I feel helpless. Victor lies to me. He is inaccessible, oily, always smiling. He does not move—progress or regress". In order to illustrate how Victor was keeping a "border" between himself and his analyst, Dr. Adeline told me about Victor's new habit: he would go to the bathroom before and after each session. He told the analyst that he had to urinate before and after lying on the couch. He then added that he had bought an audio cassette with the sound of water running. Apparently he had begun listening to the sound of water before falling asleep. Dr. Adeline recalled how Victor had difficulty urinating before his circumcision and wondered if Victor's new habit had a connection to it. Victor would not connect his wrapping himself—in a sense, with urine and putting water between himself and the external world in order to fall asleep—to his traumatic surgery. Dr. Adeline thought that Victor's new habit was his way of creating an island for himself surrounded by water. She imagined this as the new version of Victor's glass bubble. Sometime before this, she had read my description of a patient with a narcissistic personality organisation who had a fantasy of being Robinson Crusoe *without* Man Friday (Volkan, 2006b). This patient's glass bubble primarily expressed itself by his imagining himself alone on a land surrounded by water. I believe that reading the story of this patient was a factor in Dr. Adeline's noting that Victor was also creating a lonely kingdom surrounded by water and not allowing his analyst to step ashore. Dr. Adeline even thought of Victor imagining her couch as an island. She told me: "As long as I do not interfere, Victor feels safe on the couch".

Around this time there was news in the German media of a trial of a man in England who had killed his wife while in a dissociative state. This external event initiated a new preoccupation for Victor: he was afraid that he might harm his wife during his dissociative state. He allowed the analyst to see his anxiety. One morning Victor found out that the glass of his bedroom window was broken. He realised that at night, while in a different world, he had done this. The next night Victor went to Mariel's room and rapped her head with his knuckles—no damage was done. When he came to his session he appeared anxious. Talking about what he had done over the two previous nights, he remembered aspects of his dissociative state—again the encapsulation was cracked. He told Dr. Adeline that he recalled being in a bus or truck, in a dream state, and that he had been in danger of being suffocated. He needed to break the window of the bus in order to breathe and survive. Victor's being in an enclosed bus facing suffocation now reminded Dr. Adeline of the Nazis' euthanasia programme that targeted mentally ill persons, "defective" individuals. They were put in a bus, an enclosed space, into which the exhaust pipe had been directed so that gas coming from the pipe would kill everyone inside.

This session hit a very sensitive place in Dr. Adeline. All along she knew that her focusing on Victor's childhood, his parents' mourning, their withdrawal from him, their denying his psychological issues, his separation-individuation difficulties, traumatic surgeries, and his evolving grandiose self were not enough to fully understand Victor's dissociative state, especially the self- and object images, fantasies, tasks, and affects included in it. Something was missing. Dr. Adeline realised that during their very first meeting Victor had told her that his paternal grandfather had been an important Nazi figure in Berlin, in *Reichskanzlei des Führers*. Dr. Adeline knew that when Victor was a child his parental grandfather was presented to him as a "martyr", a nice person. Now she knew what this missing "something" was: information about and examination of Victor's SS officer grandfather's image in Victor's family dynamics and its impact on little Victor.

Dr. Adeline was a German person and had her own personal experiences with her father who, as a young person, had belonged to *Hitlerjugend* (Hitler Youth), and who later had served in the army during the Third Reich. Her father was not involved in any war crimes, but after the war he avoided talking about the Nazi period. Dr. Adeline was aware that her father had an obsessive orientation at home and at his business place and most of the time he behaved like a sergeant in the army. Dr. Adeline's father had died shortly after she started working with Victor. Was this a factor for her not thinking of Victor's SS officer grandfather earlier?

Dr. Adeline recalled noticing parental World War II images that had been transferred to some of her patients and that such images played a role in these patients' internal worlds. She wondered why she had not paid attention to the same topic in Victor's case until now. Besides losing her own father shortly after starting to work with Victor, she also thought of her own training psychoanalysis with a Jewish-German psychoanalyst and how she and her analyst never focused in depth on Holocaust-related issues. Were her past transference feelings about her own analyst, which were not worked through, reflected in her "countertransference" reactions to Victor, and did this cause her to avoid the Third Reich images in Victor's analysis? I was an occasional consultant for Dr. Adeline and someone she shared information with about her "difficult patient", but I did not ask for more information about Dr. Adeline's background and psychology outside of what she volunteered to tell me. Besides wondering about her own psychological issues that might be inhibiting her, she also evaluated how her patient himself did not refer to his paternal grandfather after the day of their first meeting. Obviously Victor knew his grandfather's name, but had no awareness, it seemed, of his exact position in the Third Reich.

Dr. Adeline recalled how Victor had told her that shortly after he became the "Firefighter" at age eleven he became fascinated by Edgar Allan Poe's story of a dead man whose heart would not stop beating. Poe's *The Tell-Tale Heart* was published in 1843 in the *Boston Pioneer* and revised into its current form for an 1845 edition of *The Broadway Journal*. The story involves an unnamed narrator who insists that he is sane and lives with an old man who has a clouded, pale blue eye, like a vulture's eye. The old man's horrible eye distresses the narrator and he decides to kill the man. To that end, the narrator enters the old man's room with a lantern after midnight for seven nights, but the man's eye is always closed. Without seeing the "vulture-eye" the narrator feels that he cannot kill the older man. When he enters the old man's room on the eighth night he startles the old man who awakens and sits up in his bed. The light from the lantern falls on the "vulture-eye" and the narrator pushes the old man out of his bed. He places the bed covers on top of the man and smothers him to death. The old man's heart continues beating for many minutes. The narrator then carefully cuts up the victim's body in a tub and hides all the body parts under the floorboards. Three policemen arrive at four o'clock in the morning because a neighbour reported a scream. The narrator tells the policemen that he screamed while he was sleeping and adds that the old man is out of town. He maintains his innocence until he hears a noise like the ticking of a clock. Even though no one else hears it, he perceives the noise as growing louder, and the narrator realises that it is the sound of the old man's beating heart. The narrator confesses the murder and tells the police where to find the old man's body.

Dr. Adeline thought that Victor's paternal grandfather's heart was still beating. She remembered the first time she met Victor and saw his business card with his name in small letters, almost hidden below his boss' name, as if under floorboards. He had reversed the situation in Poe's story and surrendered to the older boss' influence. Dr. Adeline recalled how proud and happy Victor had been about working for this man, the head of the "best" finance company. She sensed that Victor's grandfather's image always accompanied Victor to his sessions. Now she called me and gave me this crucial information.

Dr. Adeline too, knew Victor's grandfather's name, but did not know what he had done at *Reichskanzlei des Führers*. During our consultation she told me that she wanted to find out more about her patient's paternal grandfather before bringing to Victor's attention what she had been thinking ever since he told her of the dream and his dream-like state in which he sensed danger. She wanted to explore with Victor the links between the grandfather's image in the family dynamics and within Victor himself and Victor's evolving as a "saviour" of a "defective" brother, his sense of facing danger, moving the mattress of his bed, or breaking the glass of his bedroom window after midnight, among other related issues. Dr. Adeline wanted to go to a library and find out whatever she could about Victor's paternal grandfather. Should she do this? I wholeheartedly encouraged Dr. Adeline to do so.

CHAPTER SIX

The T4 euthanasia programme

After spending time in a library reading history books and examining documents, Dr. Adeline found out a great deal of information about Victor's paternal grandfather. He had been an important figure in the euthanasia programme, the so-called "T4 operation", the "mercy killing" of mentally and physically *defective* persons who were considered "useless" and/or presented a threat to Aryan purity in Nazi Germany. T4 is an abbreviation for *Tiergartenstraße 4*, the address of the programme's headquarters in Berlin. The T4 operation was a subsection of *Führerhauptquartier*, which was under Hitler's direct control.

According to National Socialist propaganda, the following event initiated the T4 programme: in late 1938 Hitler received a letter from the father of a boy who was blind and physically and mentally disabled asking permission to carry out the mercy killing of his handicapped son. Hitler asked his own family physician, Dr. Karl Brandt, to evaluate this petition, and in July of 1939 this child was put to death. Historians refer to this event as the beginning of the T4 programme. Three weeks after the boy was murdered Hitler authorised the creation of *Reichsausschuss zur wissenschaftlichen Erfassung erb- und anlagebedingter schwerer Leiden* (The Reich committee for the scientific registering of serious hereditary and congenital illnesses). Führer Chancellery director Phillipp Bouhler became the administrative head of this committee. He, Dr. Karl Brandt, SS-Oberführer (senior colonel) Victor Brack, police inspector Christian Wirth, and others organised the secret killing of handicapped children. Later the programme expanded to include "useless" juveniles up to seventeen years of age. Six killing centres were established and the killings were carried out by doctors or policemen (Lifton, 1986; Proctor, 1988). There were about four hundred persons who were assigned to the T4 programme. Some were commissioned to encourage parents and physicians to co-operate with the programme, and soon killing mental patients spread to occupied western Poland where the killing of "disabled" adults began as well. Some sources inform us that at first killings were mostly by lethal injection. Then it was discovered that gassing the victims was more practical. Killing people in locked trucks or busses made disposal of them quick and efficient.

The German-Soviet Non-aggression Pact (also known as the Molotov-Ribbentrop Pact), which divided eastern Europe into German and Soviet spheres of influence, was signed just before the beginning of World War II, on 23 August 1939. In September of 1939 Germans invaded western Poland, and Russians invaded eastern Poland. The annexation of the Baltic Republics by the Soviet Union took place in August of 1941. The German-Soviet Nonaggression Pact no longer existed after Nazi Germany attacked the Soviet Union without warning on 22 June 1941. From October 1939 until the spring of 1940 there was gassing in busses and mass shootings by the SS of the mentally handicapped who were hospitalised in order to create space in Germany and/or the annexed part of Poland for about 60,000 Germans who were escaping from Baltic countries that had fallen under Soviet influence.

Since thousands of doctors, nurses, and others were involved in the T4 programme, it was impossible to keep it a secret, and the population soon learned of it. Many families took their handicapped loved ones from institutions back into their homes. More importantly there was opposition to the programme from Catholic and Protestant Churches. The T4 programme was terminated in 1941, but between 1939 and 1941 an estimated 70,273 had already been murdered. Many historians saw this programme as a "rehearsal" for the "Final Solution". The T4 euthanasia programme was resumed in August 1942 and continued in secrecy throughout the last days of World War II. Testimonies collected at the Nuremberg War Tribunal, held between 20 November 1945 and 1 October 1946, indicated that about 270,000 were killed between 1939 and 1945. Since he was already dead, Victor's grandfather did not appear at the tribunal.

In order to protect Victor's identity I will not state his paternal grandfather's exact position in the T4 euthanasia programme. According to the information available in history books and documents, Victor's grandfather was assigned to another Nazi activity in 1941 when Hitler temporarily stopped the programme. I will also not name his new duty, again to protect his grandson's identity, except to say that Victor's grandfather was assigned to do things that reflected the inhumane entitlement of Nazism, although this time he was not involved in mass killings. He did not return to his position in the T4 euthanasia programme when it restarted in August 1942. He was sent to the Russian front, most likely to use his expertise to "clean up" the occupied territories from "unwanted" people such as resistant fighters and Jews. He functioned as an important SS officer—he had his own car, driver, and a nice place to live where he was served by his "host" family. There are documents illustrating that he was allowed to visit his family on several occasions before he was killed by enemy fire.

When Victor's paternal grandfather was working in the original T4 programme he and his wife had a comfortable villa in Berlin. When the Battle of Berlin was launched in November 1943, the city became a target for air raids, bombings, and mass destruction. For example, the 22 November 1943 air raid killed 2,000 Berliners and rendered 175,000 homeless. The following night there was another bombing. This time another 1,000 were killed and 100,000 made homeless. Such immense devastation would continue (Grayling, 2006).

Victor's paternal grandfather asked a rich friend to find a secure place for his wife and son, and this friend helped them move to the town where, later on, Victor was born. The friend owned a huge luxurious vacation mansion there, and Victor's grandmother and her son were given an apartment to live in; the apartment was on the third floor. Other apartments in this mansion were rented to influential people, and it had also provided a place for Hitler Youth gatherings. After moving there, Victor's paternal grandmother was involved in helping the owner manage this luxurious place. The owner was not found guilty of any Nazi crimes and continued to own this vacation house. It was not clear if Victor's grandmother started paying rent following World War II, but her son, Victor's father, grew up there and shared it with her until he married and began living in his mother-in-law's home. The reader may have already guessed that this was the place Victor moved to with Mariel after she had changed the appearance of her tattoo and for some time kept its previous connection with his family a "secret" from Dr. Adeline. While writing this book I realised that Victor and his analyst never associated Mariel's tattoo with the numbered tattoos of the Holocaust victims.

Listening to Victor, it was clear to Dr. Adeline that after World War II ended Victor's grandmother did her best to create a storyline that her husband, as an officer, had voluntarily transferred himself to a war zone, and that he was a good man and an unwilling participant in "bad things". Apparently his wife tried to establish that if her husband had survived the war he would not have been called to appear at the Nuremberg War Tribunal as a criminal.

CHAPTER SEVEN

Locked-up letters

As I learned later, Dr. Adeline did not tell Victor right away that she had found a great deal of information about his Nazi grandfather. One day when Victor was talking once more about his perception of himself as a saviour of Mariel's family's finances, the analyst saw a good opening to introduce the concept of transgenerational transmission, using layman's terms, to Victor. She told him that when he was a child he was told how his Nazi grandfather was a good man, a martyr, who had done some "bad things". She raised the possibility of Victor's being a "saviour" and doing "good things" as an attempt to correct or erase his grandfather's "bad things". If Victor knew what these "bad things" were he might find a more comfortable adjustment to his own life. At this time Victor had been seeing Dr. Adeline for more than three years, he was married, and his wife, with medical problems, was in the fourth month of her pregnancy. Responding to his analyst, once more Victor stated that he had no knowledge of his grandfather other than brief remarks he had heard about him during his childhood. Dr. Adeline continued to induce curiosity in Victor and suggested that he could find out who his paternal grandfather was and what he had done. She was not sure that Victor would look into this matter right away, but he did. He invested a great deal of time in it and, interestingly, sent all the information he found to his father. He also reported his findings to his analyst in detail, but showed no surprise or emotion. This was a big surprise to her, and Victor's strange calmness made her uncomfortable. I suggested that perhaps her emotional state was what Victor had externalised into her, that she might be owning her analysand's feelings. She kept her calm, held on to her therapeutic identity, and continued to listen to Victor.

Even though Victor had emailed the information he had found about his paternal grandfather and the T4 programme to his father, they would not talk about the SS officer at all when together. This peculiar silence between them lasted over four months. One Sunday Victor and his eight-month pregnant wife attended a barbeque party at his parents' house. Victor managed to take his father aside and confront him about what he had learned. He asked his father, face to face, about his Nazi ancestor. His father's first response was: "You are going to have a baby in a few weeks. You do not want to know". Discussing this with Dr. Adeline, Victor realised how important it had been for his paternal grandmother and his father to keep secret their connection with the big SS officer who was once close to Hitler.

When Victor was growing up there had been silence about the grandfather, but now he sensed that the paternal grandfather's image had always been there, in the family. After Victor demanded to know about his grandfather, Victor's father became ill, felt weak, and developed tinnitus. What was it that he did not wish to hear? The patient recalled how he had been told that his father had become ill when Victor was two months old. Dr. Adeline wondered if Victor's father, following his mother's death, had found documentation of his grandfather's crimes. Victor's father's illness at that time was not simply connected to a grief reaction over losing his mother; it was also connected with having a baby. If the baby, Victor, had not been healthy, the grandfather (his image) would take him into a bus and gas him. While receiving anesthesia during his surgeries Victor did not want to be gassed. The traumas of Victor's childhood surgeries were magnified by his parents' anxiety that a sick child could be murdered. This anxiety was passed on to little Victor. It was not clear why, in the long run, Richard was chosen as the "defective" child and Victor as the "saviour". Victor thought that there might have been a realistic concern about Richard's health when his brother was born. Victor's designation as the "Firefighter" was to undo the "bad things" his SS grandfather had done. However, in order to perform this task he had to be "well" and omnipotent—as omnipotent as the grandfather who was allowed to do incredibly destructive things. Such talks took place between the analyst and the patient, but Victor still did not express emotion.

One day while he was visiting his parents' home, Victor's mother admitted that there were letters that Victor's paternal grandfather had sent from the Russian front that had been kept in Victor's paternal grandmother's apartment in a secure place, locked up. After the grandmother died Victor's father brought these letters to the house where the newborn Victor had just arrived. Father kept these letters in a safe, also locking them up. In a sense, the grandfather's image had come near to baby Victor in a concrete way. Dr. Adeline wondered if the image of locked-up, encapsulated, letters might have a role in Victor's parents' passing to their son a model for a dissociative self, which Victor would later imagine as filled with chaos and disasters. Dr. Adeline tried hard to keep Victor's curiosity about the letters alive. Victor went to his father and asked to see the letters. His father said: "I will show you some of the letters. You will see that your grandfather was not a bad person. Other letters—you do not want to see them!" His father indeed gave Victor some letters and allowed him to read them. In these letters the Nazi ancestor was referring to mundane daily activities in his living space near the war zone, having potato soup prepared by a Russian woman, and so on. There were no references to the ongoing war or Nazis or their enemies. It was as if the paternal grandfather was having a pleasant vacation away from his wife and child and wished they could be with him. Only in one letter that Victor was allowed to see, did the grandfather address his son, stating clearly that if something happened to him his son should take care of his mother. In fact, after losing his father at age seven, Victor's father remained with his mother until his marriage at age thirty-five. Victor's father told his son that he did not have many actual memories of his own father and thus he did not know him. After he grew up he investigated Victor's grandfather's life once and found "nothing" important to report.

When Dr. Adeline wondered why his father would not show Victor the rest of the letters she noted that Victor himself seemed uninterested in reading them. He kept saying, "They are nothing. Why should I read more?" Most likely he was not ready to take in more "bad things". Another reason for this was that Victor's mother became very upset when she learned that he had read some of the letters and wished to read the rest. She told her son: "I am flabbergasted! I am angry. You put us on *trial*". Victor and his analyst understood that the patient's paternal grandmother, and later his father and mother, wanted to escape the humiliation and guilt that would have arisen if the SS officer ancestor had actually been put on trial.

Real events drastically interfered with the flow of Victor's work with his analyst. A month after he read some of his grandfather's letters Mariel gave birth to a boy. I will call the baby Bernd. Mariel had heavy bleeding during childbirth because the placenta had grown into the uterus muscle. This was a life-threatening situation, and Mariel underwent emergency surgery. While surgeons operated on his wife, Victor was alone in a room at the hospital, holding his newborn baby on his lap. He thought about how he had imagined that his baby might be born "defective". He was told that Bernd was healthy, but he realised that his wife's life was now in danger, or that she would live but could remain a "defective" person. He had a fleeting thought that if his wife had had an abortion she would not be facing this life-threatening situation. He imagined that abortions could be thought of as an element of euthanasia. He felt that he could not get rid of the image of his "murderer" grandfather because this new reality had once again kept the T4 programme story alive in his mind.

Mariel survived, and the surgeons were able to save her uterus too. She was offered psychological help but refused it. Mariel and her baby stayed in hospital before returning home, and during this time Victor was the primary person in the family looking after Bernd. When his wife and child came home it was clear that Mariel was in no condition to care for her baby. In reality Victor's mother-in-law and two women helpers became the primary caregivers. But Victor did not tell his analyst that Mariel and the baby were being well taken care of or about the existence of the two women helpers. Dr. Adeline could see some unexplainable confusion in Victor. She thought about Victor's experiencing an environment like the one his parents had experienced after their children were born, and the anxiety he felt about the possibility of his child being taken away from him for euthanasia. But in the sessions Victor would not verbalise his fantasies, if he was even aware of them. Only much later he would speak about his imagining that someone might damage or kill the baby. After some time passed, Victor heard his mother-in-law talking to a friend on the telephone and saying that she and Mariel did not wish to leave Bernd alone with Victor during the evening hours.

Also, because of his symptoms, everybody urged that he should never fall asleep when he was looking after the baby.

Later I learned what happened between Dr. Adeline and Victor. The analyst had an impression that Victor was overburdened by supporting his ailing wife, and she felt deeply concerned about the welfare of the newborn baby. The analyst did not know about the two women helpers. She thought that it was now a burden for Victor to drive to his analyst's office and see her three times a week. One day she found herself offering a suggestion to Victor. She asked him to consider coming to his sessions only once a week rather than three, still lying on the couch, for three months. She hoped that by that time Mariel would have regained her strength and that Victor would resume his three-hours-per-week visits. Victor hesitated, argued that analysis was going well, but after thinking about the offer he accepted it. Only a month or so later the analyst would learn that the mother-in-law had hired the two women helpers. Besides her humane and realistic wish that a newborn baby be looked after as properly as possible, psychologically speaking, she had emerged as the "saviour" of the endangered baby. But, as I will describe in the next chapter, in Victor's eyes the analytic process itself now became the "defective" object and Victor would increase his effort to be its "saviour", be his own "psychoanalyst", involved in activities to get rid of scary things within himself. After three months passed Victor refused to resume coming to see Dr. Adeline three times a week. For almost two years Victor came to see her and lay on her couch only once a week before a "routine" analytic process—this time a very different one that included a therapeutic alliance and the patient's working through his problems—would begin.

Before going further I wish to remind the reader that my aim in writing this book is to tell a story of transgenerational transmissions of past family history where the ancestor was a perpetrator connected with unbelievable human tragedies. By doing so I am also responding to Dr. Adeline's wish that such a history needed to be told, as it is an illustration of an aspect of her ethnic group's psychohistory. I am glad that I stood by her as an occasional consultant during her courageous journey with Victor. Obviously, while telling Victor's story, I will continue to make references to clinical technical issues. But it is not my intention to examine in depth Dr. Adeline's technique and my off-and-on consultations with her. Every analyst has her own personal style of conducting analysis; personal issues may intrude themselves into this style.

I am sure that if Victor underwent psychoanalytic therapy with another colleague the process of his treatment would be different. Perhaps Victor would not stay long enough with another analyst and leave the treatment. Perhaps another analyst would pay attention to the shadow of the SS officer grandfather earlier than Dr. Adeline had done, and so on. Also, if I were supervising this case in a usual manner, my role in Victor's involvement in his analytic process most likely would be different as well. I must say that I admired Dr. Adeline's tolerance and insistence on continuing to work with Victor, come rain or shine, in spite of frustrations due to his internal psychological structure and because of the Third Reich-related topics creating known or unknown hesitations in the therapeutic process.

Smiling most of the time when he was on the couch or insisting that he was "healthy"—at least for twenty hours a day—or making efforts to get "well" quickly, or keeping certain secrets were Victor's obligatory defences for survival, both psychologically (unconsciously) and physically. Such patterns were also resistance against working on his psychological problems. Even in the days of the so-called "ego psychology" (Hartmann, 1939, 1951) that dominated psychoanalytic training in the United States from 1950 to the 1980s, resistance no longer was considered an obstacle to analysis, but part of the "psychic surface", This view, I believe, was correct since resistance is an expected and "normal' phenomenon and is included—as are symptoms, inhibitions, personality traits, and adaptations—in a patient's way of dealing with mental conflicts. Resistance is not a patient's deliberate attempt to struggle with the analyst. Because every analyst also has counter feelings for and thoughts about the patient on both conscious and unconscious levels, the analyst also becomes a part of making the examination of this psychic surface easier or more difficult. In any analytic process, whatever school the analyst belongs to, there are always two persons in the room. My intention here is not to give up or minimise the psychoanalytic meaning of resistance, or the difficulties it may create, even if it belongs to a "normal" human experience. I choose to continue to utilise the term resistance. However, I do not object if someone comes up with a new term, as long as we do not lose our focus on this most crucial aspect of psychoanalysis. Dealing with resistances is required, not only at the beginning phase, but throughout the treatment.

In the T4 programme, if a physician noted that an individual was unhealthy or "defective", the physician would proclaim a death sentence on this individual. It was time, now, to explore the transference relationship, let the patient know and sense that his life was not in danger in Dr. Adeline's hands. This would help Victor develop a different kind of relatedness to the analyst, a workable therapeutic alliance. But, what happened to Mariel, and the resulting reduction of Victor's sessions from three times a week to once a week, interfered with this development.

Now let me report another event that took place between Victor and Dr. Adeline soon after Bernd was born and describe how this event, too, played a role in Victor's continuing to keep the analyst as a spectator. Victor told his analyst that he wanted to purchase new life insurance. If he died he wanted to be sure that his baby and his family would have money for their care. Apparently he informed the insurance agency that he was in treatment with a psychotherapist, and because of this he needed to get a written statement from his analyst stating that Victor was not at a higher risk of dying earlier than the average person. Dr. Adeline did not have experience in providing such paperwork for her analysands. She hesitated and then wrote and signed a statement indicating that she did not consider Victor to be in a high-risk category or his condition to be a life-threatening one. When she gave this to Victor, instead of showing his appreciation, he said, in a degrading way: "How do you know that what you wrote is true?" Perhaps the patient perceived the analyst's written statement as an indication that she would not protect him if he faced deadly danger. This was not explored.

During the next two years, coming to see Dr. Adeline regularly, but once a week, Victor would be involved in *actions*, even dramatic ones, to illustrate that he could reverse his SS grandfather's "bad" deeds. During this time period, however, he also slowly tested working together with Dr. Adeline, mostly under his control, in order to shrink and get rid of his dissociative state. More actual events in his life, which will be described later, including his being fired from his job at the finance company and separation and divorce from Mariel, were also connected with the demands of his psychological world and made the next two years of work with Victor both very frustrating but also most interesting.

CHAPTER EIGHT

Let there be oxygen

Victor filled his once-a-week sessions talking about Bernd and his care. Mariel, who had her own bedroom in the grandiose apartment, would not keep the baby by her side in the evenings because baby's every move would wake her mother. According to Victor, his mother-in-law was overtly protecting her daughter and not allowing her to slowly become a "normal mother". And, at the same time, she was not allowing Victor to be a "normal father" either. There was no curiosity in him about his mother-in-law or his wife mourning the loss of Mariel's father. Victor felt that his wife was lacking good mothering functions, not because her delivering Bernd had been traumatic and she needed recovery time from her surgery, but because of deficiencies within her psychological makeup. Dr. Adeline, and especially I, never really got to know this woman as an adult female individual with her own likes, dislikes, friends, hobbies, emotions, and ideas. I learned that she had studied art history at college, but there were no references in Victor's stories on the couch referring to arts-related activities in his wife's daily life before and during her pregnancy. Victor had considered himself a "breeding bull" and Mariel had become pregnant. Since then, apparently there had been no sexual activity between Victor and his wife.

Victor presented two types of behaviour linked with Bernd's care. In the first type, he was the "saviour" of the baby. He felt his mother-in-law was trying to keep the baby away from him. At the same time she complained about fatigue from taking care of Bernd during the evenings. When Victor felt obliged to take part in Bernd's nightly feeding and care, he developed a habit of addressing the baby: "It's only me, you can stay calm". The baby did not sleep in Victor's room, but in an adjoining one. Victor would turn on a baby monitor and as soon as he heard a noise he would go to the baby's room and take care of whatever needed to be done. When the baby was not in the adjoining room but in another place with his grandmother during the night, Victor would sometimes go into a dream state—perhaps I can call it a dissociate state without encapsulation. He would recall, in his dissociate state, feverishly looking to see that the baby was alright under his covers and not in danger of suffocating. He also would recall looking under the bed with the thought that the baby had fallen and was hurt. Sometimes he would imagine that the mattress had ended up over the baby and was smothering him. The egg did not have an extra cover. After waking up in the mornings he would realise that he could not remember things that had taken place during the time he was in his second state. For example, he would notice that he had changed the position of his bed. When putting the bed back in its regular position he would realise how difficult it was to do it alone. He needed to expend a great deal of energy. But he could not remember having expended such energy moving the bed the night before.

Victor's second type of behaviour regarding Bernd started after he and his wife went for a one-week vacation, leaving their infant behind with his mother-in-law. During the vacation both of them experienced a huge emotional gap between them, and he noted that his "love" for Mariel was gone. Victor began to think of Bernd as being like the "defective" brother of his childhood: his brother "stole" Victor's mother from him. Now Bernd had "stolen" Mariel from Victor.

The analyst tried to connect what Victor was reporting about his relationships with his son, wife, and mother-in-law to events in Victor's childhood and to the psychological influence of his SS grandfather on his family. When Victor talked about imagining the bed falling on Bernd and suffocating him, both the analyst and patient could easily see that this image also appeared in Edgar Allan Poe's *The Tell-Tale Heart* story. However, Dr. Adeline noticed Victor's lack of curiosity in joining her to explore further links between his present thoughts and activities and his childhood experiences.

According to Victor, Mariel remained "ill" by having psychosomatic symptoms. She began openly considering a separation from Victor. He considered himself as someone who did not have a place in his own apartment, and he described how Mariel was spending her days watching soap operas on television. Now Victor's weekly therapy sessions were filled with continual talk about baby's needs, emphasising that they could not be postponed or diverted. Then suddenly Dr. Adeline learned that Victor had been fired from the finance company where he had worked for many years. She had heard earlier, when he was spending so much time looking after Mariel's family's finances, how he had some problems at work. But, after Mariel's father died the family's finances were no longer problematic, mainly because there were no longer huge expenses for her father's care. Nevertheless, hearing that Victor had lost his job was a surprise to Dr. Adeline. Because he was without a job, according to Victor, Mariel postponed their separation until Bernd was one year old. Mariel, with Bernd, then moved to the city. Her mother sold her house and joined them at their new location. As I will describe later, when Bernd was two, Mariel and Victor would be divorced.

Before returning to recount what happened to Victor after his separation from his wife I will present data on how Victor tried to "remember" what was in his encapsulated egg, as well as how he found ways to "get well" by becoming involved in certain activities. By this time his analyst and I had a clear idea that when he was in his dissociated state the danger he perceived was a sense of being in a bus where he and everyone else in this bus would face suffocation. No oxygen would be available for them to breathe and stay alive. Then, again in his dissociate state, he would try to save himself and others by finding ways to get everyone out of the bus or by breaking a window in order to make oxygen available for everyone. We were also aware of Victor's grandiosity. He exhibited it during his sessions and by recollecting events such as when he was a youngster and had perceived Catholic classmates as inferior. The "chaos" that filled the encapsulated egg was an expression of his holding on to his fear of waiting to be gassed, his struggle to save people from the Nazis, all the while holding on to his superiority. The link between his superiority and his grandfather's Nazi superiority would slowly become clear in our minds. In other words, he had assimilated the grandiose image of the aggressor in order to deal with the tragic damage caused by the aggressor. Such a condition, opposite elements co-existing in the egg, certainly would be perceived as a "chaos" or "catastrophe".

Dr. Adeline learned another of Victor's "secrets". This one was connected with Victor's desire to own the big house that had the third-floor apartment he was renting and living in alone. The reader can recall that the apartment was the place where Victor's father and paternal grandmother came to live after they had left Berlin. Their coming to this apartment was connected with Victor's paternal grandfather's superiority, his being a big-shot SS officer. The original owner, a very rich German, wanted to please his friend, Victor's grandfather. This man was long dead and his descendants had sold this huge building to a rental management company to which Victor was now paying very high rent for his third-floor apartment. Listening to her patient, Dr. Adeline realised that Victor's wish to own this place was primarily connected with his wish to own Nazi superiority. She learned more about a section on the first floor, which was now rented as a conference hall for various types of meetings. It was here that Hitler Youth had gathered. More importantly, on the third floor, and especially in the apartment where Victor was living, there were some paintings. In Victor's fantasy they were paintings stolen from other countries by the Nazis, given to the owner of the big house, and specifically put in the area where his paternal grandmother and his father had settled. By owning his building Victor would become like the original owner, a "boss", and take possession of the paintings, like a rich Nazi sympathiser who was entitled to own them. At the same time he had fantasies of renting apartments in this huge building, after buying it, to people with children and putting up the "best" children's playground in the garden. Then he would watch children play. He was not aware that by creating a playground he wanted to reverse his superior grandfather's deeds, and instead of killing children he would provide them with a happy life without fear. Victor had kept his primary motivation for renting the third floor apartment and his deep desire to buy it as a "secret" from his analyst until now. Buying this big building was absolutely unrealistic, a fantasy motivated by Victor's internal world. It was a symbolic expression of the opposing elements of his dissociative state: to be as special as a Nazi big shot versus removing guilt feelings connected with murderous Nazi acts. Instead, with money borrowed from Mariel's family and his parents, and in partnership with

Mariel, he bought a much smaller building in the city and turned it into a guesthouse as one way of developing a rental business on his own.

Victor was keeping more "secrets" from his analyst. After he was fired from his job he slowly let Dr. Adeline learn about illegal activities at the finance company where he had worked prior to being fired. While administering some clients' money the company would add a zero at the end of the amount of the collected money and thus falsely multiplying the number. Then they would gamble with this false amount of money on the stock market. I am not well-versed in financial matters and I cannot exactly describe for the reader how the company was carrying out this illegal handling of investors' money. However, it is apparent that the "best" finance company was corrupt and the "best boss" a criminal. Apparently Victor went along with them; sometimes he would imagine illegal schemes and play with them in his mind, and wonder if his boss would consider utilising them. He never shared what came to his mind with anyone. However, I heard an echo in this story of Victor's SS grandfather considering Hitler as the "best boss", and volunteering to be involved in inhumane activities. What was interesting at this time was Victor's stating that the "good name" of his boss, under which he had hidden his own name on the business card he had presented to his analyst on his first visit, was really a "made up" name to illustrate power and superiority. Victor wanted to move away from his criminal boss with the hope that, in the future, he would find his own customers and deal with them in a non-criminal fashion.

Before he was fired, Victor had been the primary person in a special business venture on behalf of the finance company. When Dr. Adeline heard about it she recognised it as a most clear symbolic expression of Victor's internal demand to save people in a bus at risk of being gassed by the Nazis. Sometime before, Victor was talking with a rich client of the company, who spoke of his daughter who was involved in ecological issues and who was getting ready to attend a meeting in Berlin where policymakers, environmental NGOs, and business representatives would discuss the British Climate Change Act and the legal feasibility of adopting a climate change act in Germany. What interested Victor were the customer's remarks about increasing the oxygen in the air that people would breathe in Germany. Without knowing why, for many months Victor followed the news of the establishment of the Climate Protection Act for Germany and efforts to implement special wetland restoration and save the climate by meeting greenhouse gas emission reduction targets. Ninety per cent of the huge amount of money required for renaturation of a target area, an everglade, would come from the European Union and ten per cent of the money from other sources. Victor noted that such projects would also stimulate the economy and that there would be opportunities to invest money in them. He was interested in how renaturation of an everglade might attract tourists. Kilometres-long wooden pathways over the everglade could be built; tourists walking on them would enjoy the diversity of vegetation and breathe fresh air. Victor toured some of the target areas and got people to invest money in his finance company with the idea of using it for the ten per cent of the money that was required for the work in these areas. In turn, with increased tourism the investors would regain the money they had invested in this project and more. He would not need to break a window in his dissociate state; he was finding oxygen when he was not in a dissociated state. He had even invested his family's money in this venture. It was at this time that Victor fully realised how the "best" boss anybody could have was stealing money from the customers, including those involved in the climate protection project. Victor was fired.

Following his dismissal from the finance company and separation from his wife, Victor behaved as a man with "acute paranoia". He copied thousands of emails belonging to the finance company and put them on a hard disk, took the hard disk with him out of the company's building, and hid it. His idea was to have evidence to illustrate his innocence if the company came under legal investigation. He also erased some files on the company's main computer in order to get rid of material that might be self-incriminating. He repeated that persons could be killed for doing less than what he had done, and he felt that his life was in danger. He was afraid to leave the place where he was staying. When somebody rang the doorbell he would feel anxious. In fact he went into hiding, both physically and electronically, by not doing anything on his computer that might provide information to any person searching for his whereabouts. He kept visiting Dr. Adeline once a week.

During the first year following Victor's seeing Dr. Adeline once a week I did not hear from her much. Once she wrote to me and stated that she was feeling as if she were "castrated" by Victor, as Victor was "castrated" by circumcision at age eleven. But, she added, in her own English, that she was "potent" during the whole week except when she was with Victor for fifty minutes and then she felt "handicapped".

I noted an echo in her writing of Victor's repeated statement that he was healthy all day and night except for four early morning hours. I thought Victor was utilising his analyst to deposit some aspects of himself into, while, through his actions, was trying to "get well".

Apparently Victor came out of his "acute paranoia" after two months or so. I do not know if there was an event that helped him to move out of hiding. Dr. Adeline recalled how he came to one of his sessions and declared that there was no necessity for him to be afraid and that his "horniness" had returned. He talked to a lawyer, hired him, and sued the finance company for firing him and also for recovery of his parents' money that he had invested in the firm. I will describe his court appearances in the next chapter. The trials kept Victor's involvement in the finance company, and especially in the everglade project, alive in his mind. He became able to work with Dr. Adeline and realise and own his psychological motivation for the climate protection project. By removing the climate killer CO_2 and at the same time producing oxygen in the air, Victor was dealing with his grandfather's "guilt feelings" about his role in depriving innocent people of oxygen. He truly sensed that the image of his ancestor had been deposited in him along with tasks to turn the older man's "bad deeds" into good ones.

CHAPTER NINE

Legal redress and the psychology of remembering through actions

The SS grandfather was not at the Nuremberg trials of 1945 and 1946. Nor was he tried *in absentia*, like Hitler's private secretary Martin Bormann, who was tried and convicted. Victor learned that his paternal grandmother had insisted again and again that there were no reasons in the world for her husband to appear at the Nuremberg trials. It was also clear that she was afraid that sooner or later her dead husband could still face a court trial *in absentia*, even though Victor's ancestor's death had been confirmed. She and her son, Victor's father, seemed determined to hide the SS officer's "bad deeds". In the last chapter I described how Victor's mother had developed a similar attitude, as demonstrated when she learned about Victor wishing to read more of the letters from his grandfather that were kept locked up, and had accused her son of wanting to put the family "on trial". I talked with Dr. Adeline for a long time after Victor sued his former finance company. As soon as I heard about Victor's taking his "criminal" boss to court I expected to learn that this trial also stood for Victor's grandfather's trial that never actually happened.

Victor was suing the finance company for two reasons: first, to receive money equaling more than a year's salary that he would have earned had he continued working for them. He was claiming that he had been fired unjustly and that the company owed him severance pay. Second, he wanted to recover his parents' money that had been invested in the company. Therefore, there would be two trials. Dr. Adeline learned that when Victor was fired he had to borrow large amounts of money both from his parents and from his mother-in-law. After separating from his wife, the loan from his mother-in-law had become a big problem. She was telling her friends that Victor owed her money and such public knowledge would not be good for Victor as he attempted to start his own business and find clients. To Victor's horror, she also informed her friends about Victor's early-morning symptoms. Nevertheless, Victor helped his mother-in-law sell her big house. Even though Victor made some money for his mother-in-law by helping her with this sale, he was concerned she would continue to gossip about him; he wanted to be financially secure, let people know this, and have no obstacles to starting his own business.

After the separation from her husband Mariel moved to a roomy apartment in the city with Bernd, where her mother joined them. Soon Mariel found a job at a museum and her mother became Bernd's primary caregiver. Victor started to send monthly cheques to Mariel for childcare. The amount was rather high, but Victor wanted Bernd's needs to be met perfectly. He was allowed to take his son to his apartment at the weekend.

Someone at the finance company was able to restore the files that Victor had erased earlier. No one would know what he had done before leaving his job. As the first trial continued, Dr. Adeline noted that Victor was not handling himself as well as he might in the courtroom. One day Victor referred to the trial as a "phantom trial". Upon this, Dr. Adeline told Victor that he was taking his SS grandfather—along with his boss and himself—to court *in absentia*, but he needed also to keep in mind the *realities*, because he was doing things that might open the door for him to be accused as a co-criminal.

Dr. Adeline's intervention was very important, and throughout the first trial Victor kept his analyst's warning in mind and protected himself. The first trial lasted for some months. Victor received a sum of money from the finance company; it was not the exact amount he had wanted, but it covered his one-year salary. His lawyer was delighted with the compromise. It is interesting that after the court's decision was announced, when Victor saw his former boss sitting outside the courtroom, he sat next to him and they had a civilised, man-to-man conversation. He told the older man that they could have reached a compromise earlier without going to court. This illustrated a positive change in Victor. The second trial lasted much longer than the first. Victor worked closely with his parents, arguing the reasons they should receive their money back from the finance company, and, most importantly, encouraged his father to stand up firmly in court. They would win. Later Dr. Adeline told me that the second trial was like Victor and his father had got together and mastered transgenerationally transmitted trauma.

Let me return to the time when Dr. Adeline made her intervention and reminded her patient to pay attention to realities while in court; she had added that a courtroom was a very different place from an analyst's office. Dr. Adeline's remarks also opened a way for Victor to join her and examine the psychological connections of his actions, without fear of losing the realistic aims of the two trials. Some external events, too, initiated the patient's associations to the Nazi period of history and helped him to gain more insights into the connections between his going to the court and his internal psychological issues.

The first external event was the news that thirty old men in Germany had just been accused of Nazi crimes. Victor said: "If my grandfather was alive surely he too would be accused, convicted, and sentenced. It was a most evil crime to cause the murder of thousands of innocent persons". Another external event took place in the Middle East where people, including children, were gassed. Victor kept looking at the dead children's pictures on the Internet. He reported feeling shocked. Once, while on the analyst's couch, he had a brief auditory hallucination and heard a child scream in the street. Around this time he went to see a film that depicted the time of slavery in the United States. The film illustrated how African-Americans were treated as if they were less than human beings. This third external event induced Victor to connect the horrible racism in the United States with the Nazis' treatment of Jewish and Romani people, as well as "defective" children and adults. It was painful for Victor. Dr. Adeline told me later how all of the above developments were also very difficult for her to hear and tolerate. Both the patient and the analyst were in a very uncomfortable emotional state while keeping their enquiring minds functional. One day Victor, in frustration, spoke loudly and declared that he wanted to get out of his uncomfortable state. He recalled the film dealing with racism and thought he might be like white people in the United States. The film, as if it was day residue, was instrumental in Victor noticing that besides his psychological task to reverse his grandfather's "bad deeds" he was also holding on to the myth of his grandfather's Nazi superiority.

When I heard Victor's associations to the film some months later, I wondered if his breaking glass during his dissociative state might also have a link to *Kristallnacht*. On 7 November 1938, a Jewish teenager, Herschel Grynszpan, fatally shot a German diplomat in Paris. A co-ordinated anti-Jewish pogrom took place in the German Reich, especially in Berlin and Vienna, on 9 and 10 November 1938. Storm troopers, Hitler Youth, and German civilians vandalised and broke the windows of synagogues, and Jewish-owned shops and homes; broken glass littered the streets. The event was named "The Night of Crystal" in the Third Reich, turning the horror of breaking glass into the image of nice crystal. It is beyond this book's aim to provide details of this event except to note that an estimated 30,000 Jewish males were arrested and sent to concentration camps. This was the first time such a huge number of Jews had been incarcerated on the basis of their ethnicity. Many scholars referred to *Kristallnacht* as a turning point in National Socialist anti-Semitic policy (see, for example, Gilbert, 2006; Read, 1989; and Steinweis, 2009). I was sure that Victor had grown up hearing about *Kristallnacht*. If his egg included influences of both his wish to break glass to obtain oxygen and to do the same thing to feel like a Nazi, certainly "chaos" would be present. I wanted to talk about what had come to my mind with Dr. Adeline. But, I knew that at this time she too was having a hard time due to many Nazi-related reminders coming into her office. Much later she and I talked about the idea of Victor's breaking glass including *Kristallnacht* symbolism. She told me that *Kristallnacht* had not come up directly during her work with Victor.

When he first came for treatment Victor had an encapsulated dissociative state, an egg with an extra shell under his arm. He, as the "Firefighter", was involved in many actions ranging from his preoccupation with the analyst's little rug, to daily calling Richard, to his marrying Mariel and working on her family finances. The primary aim of these actions was to keep the egg isolated and safe from being broken. His involvement in the everglade project still primarily reflected the main aim of his daily activities. His suing the finance company and his associations connected with court activities led him to sense and observe the "chaos" within the egg. The egg contained a mixture of images, unconscious fantasies, and feelings: images of anxious parents with secrets, his grandfather, Nazis, surgeons, Catholic boys. It contained fantasies about what such images could do to him and in turn what he could do against them and how he could save himself and others from them; and there were feelings of pain, guilt, shame, as well as a sense of grandiosity. The intertwining of such images, unconscious fantasies, and feelings created high tension that had to be encapsulated at least twenty hours a day, while he needed to allow for a discharge of tension for only four hours each day. During twenty hours of the day he needed to be involved in actions that demonstrated a healthy, self-sufficient man and a saviour. No one would see his hidden "chaos" and perceive him as "defective". He would not face situations such as his childhood surgeries and Catholic boys' aggression, and no Nazi would ever consider gassing him. Such dangerous possibilities were locked away in the egg, which had its own separate life for a few hours after midnight. For some time now Victor had been allowing himself, in Dr. Adeline's presence, to sense what was in the egg and to experience mixed emotions linked to its content. I will write about his referring to breaking the eggshell in the next chapter.

Otto Fenichel (1945) summarised the classic psychoanalytic view of action as something that "impedes the ego from being confronted with unconscious material" (p. 570). He argued that an activity "relates only to the present and does not make the patient conscious of being dominated by his past. Analysis should show the past to be effective in the present" (p. 571). Fenichel was referring to an adult patient's acting out (outside the analyst's office) or acting in (within the sessions). These terms refer to expression "through action, rather than words of a memory, an attitude, or a conflict by a person in psychoanalysis or another form of treatment that is based on verbalization" (Moore & Fine, 1990). Freud (1914) stated that acting out could be a way of remembering, but explored more how it served as a resistance against treatment. Classical analysts considered it an undesirable concept and patients' actions were not frequently studied or mentioned in the psychoanalytic literature.

I consider Alan Wheelis as the pioneer in acknowledging the role of action in resolving intrapsychic problems (Wheelis, 1950). While he was telling analysts to pay attention to certain actions of their patients, Wheelis was not devaluing the need to work through in the analytic process with words. And, it is important to note that he warned analysts not to persuade their patients to act in any certain way. His paper, in general, did not make an impact on psychoanalytic practice. During a 1967 panel discussion at the International Psychoanalytic Congress in Copenhagen, Leo Rangell "liberated" acting out from its previously pejorative bias. He pointed out its communicative nature and value in treatment. The paper he gave at this congress on this topic was published a year later (Rangell, 1968). The same year Samuel Novey presented his concept, called "the second look", about actions involved in visiting childhood locations, old scenes, in the interest of mastering the past. He stated that he borrowed this thesis from Freud who "advanced the view that children repeat unpleasurable experiences so that they can actively master the situation which they had first experienced passively" (Novey, 1968, p. 71). Warren Poland (1977) and I (Volkan, 1979) described a phenomenon, pilgrimage, that is similar to Novey's concept of the second look. Meanwhile Harold Blum wrote that "acting out", in its classical sense, is a formidable resistance, but patient's actions "may also represent efforts to master trauma, and a transference development coincident with analytic work and a step toward sublimated activity" (Blum, 1976, p. 183).

My interest in patients' actions while in psychoanalytic treatment evolved when I put individuals who did not have adequately integrated self-representation on my couch. The primary therapeutic aim was to bring them to a level where they would attempt to mend the splitting or fragmentation in their personality organisation. I noted that words describing such mending processes were not enough for them. They had to become involved in certain types of actions so they could actually experience the structural change within themselves and own this change. I referred to such actions as "therapeutic play". In therapeutic play, the "play" is not described in words, but is primarily expressed in specific activities that typically continue for weeks or months. The patient's preoccupation with and reporting of this action to the analyst becomes the central focus of verbal communication from session to session. The therapeutic play comes to an end in a way that is a new experience for the patient internally. I also noted therapeutic play of patients with higher level personality organisation. In their cases the aim was not to experience mending, but owning the resolution of a difficult mental conflict or taming the pathological influence of an unconscious fantasy. One young man's penis was injured when he was at the oedipal age and also during adolescence. His fantasy of being castrated was actualised and also created mental conflicts. After he understood the impact of his childhood traumas on him he was involved in therapeutic play.

When his new job required his riding a bicycle, first he bought a damaged bicycle that represented the image of his damaged penis. Then he acquired a super bicycle that represented the opposite of a damaged penis, a defensively powerful penis image between his legs. The last phase of his actions was to acquire a "normal" bicycle. Therapeutic play took him many months before there was a positive result. By his actions he "learned" that he could be an average individual, a well person. In short, I became aware of actions' different roles and appreciated those that were essential for analysands who were reaching towards a more adaptive, healthy level of functioning (Volkan, 1987, 2004b, 2010; Volkan & Ast, 2001; Volkan, Ast, & Greer, 2002; Volkan & Fowler, 2009).

The actions Victor exhibited both inside and outside his analyst's office during the first years of his treatment can be considered acting out in its classical sense. His involvement in the project to pump more oxygen into the air, and especially in the court trial, was similar to therapeutic play. Victor was in need of a "new object" (sometimes called "analytic object", or "developmental object") (Cameron, 1961; Giovacchini, 1972; Kernberg, 1975; Loewald, 1960; Tähkä, 1993; Volkan, 1976; Volkan & Ast, 1992, 1994) to internalise and identify with in order to replace pathological identifications from his original childhood experiences and from what had been deposited in him. The patient's interaction with a "new object" is akin to a nurturing child-mother relationship (Ekstein, 1966; Rapaport, 1951). To illustrate such a need would be dangerous for Victor since it would portray him as a weak individual, the opposite of his main defensive position as self-sufficient and grandiose. Thus he hid his need for a "new object" by his activities, including those on the couch, his "self-analysis". However, his need for a "new object" made him continue coming to Dr. Adeline's office, but under his control, as we saw in his refusal to resume his three-times-a-week routine. Dr. Adeline's countertransference response, I think, was frustration. When Victor's actions began to assume aims of therapeutic play Dr. Adeline found herself having more empathy for Victor and feeling that she was no longer a spectator watching an Olympic runner run. She and Victor were arriving at a location where they would walk together side by side. Further examination of the contents of his egg and his dealing with the egg would be possible with his bringing other actions to his analyst's attention, such as his becoming a photographer.

CHAPTER TEN

Photography, maggots, and jumping over a barbed wire fence

While the trials were taking place, and after they ended, Victor exhibited involvement in two new types of repeated actions. In the first, he put hard sweets in his mouth during his sessions and sucked on them. The second was his hobby of taking photographs at many locations. His actions reminded me of two of my patients.

The first patient who came to my mind was a young woman who had been an unwanted baby. She had a very narcissistic mother who was very upset because her pregnancy had left wrinkles on her abdomen. In the mornings her mother would stand naked in front of a big mirror, look at her wrinkles, feel frustrated, and then call her maid to take care of her baby while she went to a corner and sulked. When this patient began seeing me, in her mind, I was an archaic "bad object", a "bad mother". She did not wish to "take me in". A few months after we started her treatment I noted that while she was on my couch she had something in her mouth. I learned that before each session she secretly put a "Life Saver" in her mouth. Life Saver is the name of certain peppermint sweets sold in small packages in the United States. By her actions this woman would prevent the intrusion of a dangerous analyst image representing her early mother from entering into her (Volkan, 2010). By putting a sweet in his mouth Victor was trying to do the opposite of what my analysand tried to do. Victor was expressing a wish to take in, introject, a sweet "new object" (also referred to in the literature as "analytic object", or "developmental object") (Loewald, 1960; Cameron, 1961; Giovacchini, 1972; Kernberg, 1975; Volkan, 1976; Tähkä, 1993; Volkan & Ast, 1992, 1994). The analyst's newness does not refer to her social existence in the real world, but depends on the analyst being an object (and its representation) not hitherto encountered. Victor was expressing a wish to take in the "new object", identify with it, and develop new and healthier ego functions. One day on the couch he pointed to himself and said: "Free yourself from fears, live up to your dreams". I think that the analyst's "introject" was talking to Victor. He reported going swimming for the first time in years and losing the weight he had gained while living with Mariel. Referring to the trials he asked: "From where did my courage to go through it come from?" Then he listed his grandfather's tasks involved in euthanasia activities and other illegal, inhumane things he had done, and compared them with what he had done himself at the finance company and what he wanted to do in the future. Already he was giving examples of some internal changes.

The second patient who came to my mind was one of my first analysands, also a young woman. I had worked with her decades ago. At the time of her birth, her older sister, who was one and a half, was ill and expected to die. Her mother, who was experiencing an anticipated mourning, had a breast infection. Because of pain, while feeding my patient she would often suddenly pull her nipple away from my patient's mouth. The sister died before my patient was two years old. Her father, frustrated with his wife's years of persistent mourning, slowly began handling his second child sexually, until she reached puberty. Thus, my patient was also traumatised by incest. A year or so after she started to see me, after each of her sessions was over, she would sit on my couch for a minute, look at me, and blink her eyes. Then she would leave my room. She informed me that by blinking her eyes she was taking my picture. Between her sessions, when she felt overwhelmed by bad feelings she would go to a dark room and blink her eyes again. At this time, in her mind, my pictorial image would be reflected on a flat surface. Sensing my presence next to her would calm her down. For her I had become a "new object". Through "taking me in" she would keep my "introject" within her, and by externalising it next to her she would manage difficult situations (Volkan, 2002). At that time she had not yet identified fully with my image as a "new object".

I thought that Victor's photography hobby was connected with his wish to take in his analyst's image, as my first analysand symbolically had done. Before Victor could do this, he was taking pictures of externalised "bad objects". By describing such images to his analyst, Victor was attempting to modify and rid himself of these "bad objects", thereby making space for the "new object". Apparently there was a place in the city where Dr. Adeline lived called the Slaughter House District. In several buildings in one large area within this district butchering animals was still taking place. Apparently a passerby could smell the blood and hear the animals screaming. Other buildings were used as packaging houses preparing the meat for sale. A neighbouring area, still within the Slaughter House District, had been renovated and turned into a shopping centre that included a restaurant, fruit markets, and a cinema. Without being aware of his internal psychological motivations, Victor became fascinated with taking pictures in the Slaughter House District and excited about describing his photographs to his analyst. Soon Dr. Adeline realised that the Slaughter House District stood for Nazi locations where innocent persons had been killed; butchered animals stood for innocent "defective individuals", Jewish and Romani persons. But since it was possible to turn a bloody place into a shopping centre with stores selling beautiful things, entertainment places, and restaurants, and fill it with happy, laughing, alive people, Victor, too, could change his horrible images connected with his Nazi grandfather into unfrightening ones. Dr. Adeline explained to Victor what this, as well as having a sweet in his mouth, meant. He began walking with his analyst, symbolically speaking, side by side and examined what he had been told. He began gaining real insights.

One Monday morning after parking his car near Dr. Adeline's office, as expected, he passed by a skip. In this nice neighborhood this rubbish container was kept closed and its surrounding area very clean. Apparently someone had put a huge piece of meat in the dumpster over the weekend and forgotten to cover it. The rotten meat smelled terrible and maggots were feasting on it. Victor started his session by referring to what he had just seen. Dr. Adeline knew that what her patient was describing was not a hallucination; an hour earlier she too had passed by this skip. During this hour and many hours that followed this one, Victor continually referred to maggots, thinking of maggots eating the flesh of victims killed by the Nazis. An image came to his mind: a bus with no windows filled with corpses. A man with a hammer was trying to nail the bus to the ground so it could not move, while a mean-looking woman with a broom swept the ground around the bus. Victor recalled that a long time ago, when he was describing his "cloud" images, Dr. Adeline had suggested that he draw a picture of his "clouds" so that she could better visualise what he was referring to. Victor never drew the picture for his analyst. Now, when his analyst was away for a week attending a professional meeting, the windowless bus with two persons working around it became like a "postcard" in Victor's imagination. He had not taken a photograph of the rotten meat covered with maggots, but in his mind he had drawn a picture associated with what he had seen. He had a fantasy of sitting next to Dr. Adeline on a hilltop, looking down and watching what was depicted on his "postcard". The image of the man nailing the bus into the ground was associated with the image of Victor's parents who had nailed Victor's Nazi grandfather's image into their son's mind. The image of the mean-looking woman sweeping the ground became the image of the paternal grandmother/mother/father who was denying and hiding the events that had taken place in busses during the Nazi times. The important thing was Victor's sitting next to his analyst and their watching his "postcard" together.

During the next sessions Victor "saw" that the bus was full of corpses. Then he thought that even though they were dead, they would not have decomposed in Nazi times because the maggots that would be necessary for this process must also have been killed by the gas. But then, one day, Victor imagined that the analytic couch was being attacked by hundreds of maggots while he was lying on it. He sensed that maggots were touching his skin and eating him up. He had brought his fear of being killed, as well as his "postcard", into the analytic office. Soon the meaning of what he really wanted to do by bringing the maggots to the analyst's couch—his wish to move the bus from his mind—appeared. He started talking about the execution of murderers in the United States. Always two people would push buttons at the same time to execute the criminal by electrocution so that no one would know who had actually performed the killing. Two people would share this task. Dr. Adeline told Victor that he and she together were "killing" his murderer SS grandfather's representation that had been deposited in Victor. This, in turn would free Victor. He sensed internally, understood, and accepted this interpretation. He had brought maggots to the analyst's couch so they would eat up the representation of his grandfather *within* him. During a later session, Victor imagined rats eating maggots.

He developed another picture in his mind of a soldier dying and rats waiting to eat him too. After this session, he went with a woman friend to the Slaughter House District to take more photographs. When he came to his next session he told Dr. Adeline that he had seen a car next to the shopping centre with a sign that looked like a bunch of white wires. Victor described how the sign brought forth the image of a brain in his mind. Maggots began eating up the brain. A fish jumped out of the brain, went to the sea, and began swimming. Recalling how Victor had gone swimming recently, Dr. Adeline told him that the fish in his imagination represented Victor himself. He was separating himself from his grandfather's mental representation, and he had gone swimming; his coming to shore would be like a rebirth. Some time ago, when there was a break between his two trials, Victor had joined a tour group for ten days and visited some places in South America. Now he was aware of why he had taken this tour. He recalled long ago reading about Nazis escaping to South America, changing their names, and living there. He had imagined his SS grandfather lying; he was not really dead, but had gone to South America and was hiding there. Now Victor realised his motivation for touring South America. He said: "I did not find him. He is dead".

Victor became interested in examining old German photographs. One day he came across a famous photograph of an East German soldier jumping over barbed wire to West Germany as the Berlin Wall was in the process of being erected. This man escaped at the very last minute from, as Victor said, "being imprisoned in East Germany". I was curious and found this photograph myself. I saw a young man in uniform, carrying his gun, in the air, jumping over barbed wire. Since he was looking down and wearing a helmet, half of his face was covered. Because he was not recognisable, I thought it was easier for Victor to externalise his own image on to this soldier seeking freedom. On the couch, referring to the escaping soldier, Victor said: "*We* all know him". Then he wondered why such a thought had come to his mind. He mumbled: "Why did I say 'we' know him? It is nonsense! Who are 'we'? My family? My grandfather? Why my grandfather?" After a silence he declared: "It is me. I jumped to my freedom". He recalled that when he was much younger he had participated in two bicycle tours, and on both occasions he had fallen into barbed wire. "This time, I fell into freedom", he stated and added: "No more bad boss, no funds for my everglade project, no wife, no mother-in-law; and I left my son". He said that while he was jumping into freedom he was cut and bled. "Blood stained my shirt. Now I need to take care of the blood on my shirt".

In his next session he reported that he slept better after taking more pictures at the Slaughter House District. He also spoke about spending a night with a beautiful woman. Now and then Victor was dating women. Once he learned that a woman he went out with had a mentally deficient child. He told Dr. Adeline that he did not wish to be involved with this woman further since he might repeat his childhood experiences through action. Instead, he described a photograph to Dr. Adeline and talked about it. Apparently this photograph showed little Richard sitting on a tricycle smiling. Victor knew that he had been forced by his parents to give his tricycle to his brother. He addressed himself as if Dr. Adeline was within him: "Focus more on childhood, work more on it, and free yourself". He was illustrating how Dr. Adeline existed as an "introject" in him.

Victor became interested in the concept of mourning. Letting go of images and replacing them with a "new" one would require mourning. On the surface he wondered how parents could ever mourn their children who were taken away from them to be killed as the T4 programme dictated. His bonding with Bernd had started much earlier. Victor was not pleased with how Mariel and her mother were taking care of Bernd, and he also knew that his own ageing parents could not be good caretakers for his son. He wanted to go to court and demand full custody of Bernd. This was an unrealistic wish. According to an agreement with his wife, his son stayed with him two and a half days every weekend, except the one weekend when he was in South America. Being with his son was exhausting, but also fun. He had girlfriends and selected them according to their willingness to accept him as the father of a little boy. When Bernd was with him he kept any girlfriend away in order not to endanger the arrangement with Mariel. This would change after he began going steady with Lara, whose relationship with Victor will be described in the next chapter. Dr. Adeline heard how Victor was sleeping with Bernd, and there was no mention of Victor experiencing his dissociative state. This was a major development. Sometime later he reported that when he was lost in thought his son would say "Hello papa" and bring him back to the present. He was hinting at what remained from his old dissociate state.

CHAPTER ELEVEN

Searching for and finding a new life

When Bernd was about two years old Victor and Mariel were legally divorced. Victor wondered what to do with his wedding ring. Should he melt it down? Then he realised that he did not even know where he had put it. He had stopped wearing it since his separation from Mariel when he was upset to learn of her wish to return to using her maiden name and rid herself of his family name. This brought a question to Victor's mind: "Do I want to change my last name? Do I want to break my connection to my grandfather and father and my family's Nazi history?" He concluded that what would count more was establishing and maintaining a change within himself. In some of his sessions, Victor would say he had found his freedom, not only in his external life, but also internally and he was ready to finish his treatment. However, in other sessions he would talk about feeling empty. Around this time I went to Europe for a psychoanalytic congress that Dr. Adeline was also attending, and we were able to find time to review her work with Victor. Referring to Victor's remarks about his feeling empty, I suggested that more time was needed for his stable identification with the analytic object and his assimilation of new adaptive ego functions. I reminded Dr. Adeline of Victor's own statement after he identified with the photograph of the East German soldier jumping over barbed wire. Victor had stated that while he had jumped into freedom, he had cut himself and was bleeding. More work was required to clean the blood and to heal this new cut. She readily agreed with me that it was not time to consider terminating Victor's treatment.

I urged Dr. Adeline to make a new arrangement with Victor and start seeing him again three times a week. The reader may recall that Dr. Adeline had offered to see her patient once a week for *only* three months and it had been two years now. On many occasions Dr. Adeline had expressed her concern regarding this matter. Although he had made much progress and gained insights into the role played by his childhood environment, his surgeries, and transgenerational transmissions in his psychopathology, and made drastic changes working with his analyst, Victor had turned her and the analytic process into a "defective one". Under the surface, he was still relating to a "defective" object and being its "saviour", as he had "learned" to do in childhood. Beneath all his work he was holding on to his original defence/resistance by remaining his own analyst and keeping Dr. Adeline under his control. I understood that Dr. Adeline had raised questions about the frequency of Victor's sessions and each time Victor would not go along with her and the topic was postponed. Victor had to deal with many external world issues: he was fired and had to look for new ways to make money; he appeared in two trials; and he took care of Bernd at weekends. Even though his own psychology had played a role in initiating most of these challenges, I sensed that Dr. Adeline was careful not to hurt him. Perhaps she was also responding unconsciously to being put in a "defective" position and thus she was, in turn, not "correcting" Victor's analytic process as an expression of her frustration. In my mind there was also the possibility that during her work with Victor she was being subjected, unconsciously, to emotions concerning her own father's history during the Third Reich. We discussed these topics without my pushing to learn more about Dr. Adeline's very personal issues. I urged her to go back to working in a more intensive psychoanalytic way with Victor. I stated that it was time to offer a plate of enchiladas filled with variety of ingredients—cheese, chicken, pork, seafood, beans, potatoes, and vegetables—to Victor in order to prepare him for coming to see her again three times a week. She did not understand what I meant by referring to this Mexican dish, so I explained.

At the time I saw Dr. Adeline in Europe at the psychoanalytic congress, I had for some years been spending three months each year at the Austen Riggs Center in Massachusetts as the Senior Erik Erikson Scholar and attending case conferences. Many "difficult patients" who have seen several therapists and been exposed to various therapeutic approaches, ranging from talking therapies to electric shock, come to Austen Riggs. Four times a week they see an experienced analyst or therapist or a fellow still in training. Fellows in training receive regular supervision from experienced colleagues. Most of the time individuals newly admitted to the Austen Riggs Center carry what can be called a built-in transference (Volkan, 2010; Werman, 1984). That is, such individuals unconsciously relate to the present therapist or analyst as an extension of, and thus not clearly separate from, their past therapists, even if the capacity to distinguish between them intellectually is intact. The new therapist or analyst, who was not present at the patient's previous treatments, naturally has no (or very little) knowledge about the experiences, expectations, and feelings unexplored during the previous therapies, factors that may be carried into his or her work with the patient. In turn, the patient, although unaware of it, anticipates certain responses from the new therapist or analyst similar to ones received earlier from another therapist, and is puzzled when the current therapist or analyst does not behave in a particular way. Attending to indications of a built-in transference is critically important in the establishment of a solid therapeutic relationship. Also, a patient who has seen different people for help collects different "insights" that may or may not be relevant to the patient's psychopathology and may or may not be put together without confusion. While staying at Austen Riggs I began to advise the fellows to pay special attention to their new patients' built-in transferences and "insights" about their problems collected in past treatments. I told the fellows to share their findings with their new patients. This would, I hoped, help the fellows free themselves, as much as possible, from being targets of built-in transferences and separate themselves as individuals different from the other past helpers. I noted that fellows who followed my suggestions were able to develop better therapeutic alliances with their new patients. One day, I was having lunch at a Mexican restaurant with a couple of new Austen Riggs fellows and explaining to them what I described above. While we were involved in this conversation we were served plates of enchiladas. One fellow likened giving a "summary" related to built-in transference and related issues to a newly arrived patient in order to attempt to prevent a major resistance to the treatment, to presenting a plate of enchiladas with various ingredients. One has to be careful to present the right amount of "food" in order to avoid heartburn. Since then I use the term "presenting a plate of enchiladas", just the right amount, for this technical suggestion.

Victor had not sought treatment from anyone else before coming to see Dr. Adeline. However, when he started his analysis he was "two persons". On many occasions, as described in previous chapters, he remembered various aspects of his psychopathology and his attempts to deal with them through actions. While he was involved in these actions he had various "transference relationships" with individuals such as his old boss whose superior image in Victor's mind, in time, was turned into the image of a criminal. While he was involved with her, Mariel was a "defective person" whom he needed to rescue. He frequently utilised his mother-in-law as a "bad object". A person who worked at a government office and who was helpful to him in developing his environmental project was a "good object". Sometimes he was an analysand who saw his analyst three times a week and other times a patient who met with his analyst once a week. Very rich material was collected, mainly though understanding what he was doing in his actions. He had, symbolically speaking, began walking side by side with Dr. Adeline and they began observing things together. But beneath this surface he was still controlling the analytic process and holding on to being the "Firefighter".

I told Dr. Adeline to tell Victor that she had something very important to tell him and ask him to sit in front of her. Then she would make a "summary" of major insights collected and explain where they were in his treatment process. She would insist that the time had come for them to meet three times a week, and they should do this without Dr. Adeline and the analytic process remaining under Victor's "control" and without Dr. Adeline remaining as a "defective analyst", so that he could finish assimilating new ego functions and *really* get well. Dr. Adeline followed my suggestions. Later I learned that she had Victor sit in front of her not only during one session, but three. She presented him a plate of enchiladas, without overfeeding him.

By coming to see his analyst three times a week, Victor and Dr. Adeline began a new chapter in their work together. Victor began talking more and more about his new girlfriend Lara. He knew Lara from his early school days, but he had never been her boyfriend until they met by accident at a social gathering a year after he was separated from Mariel. She was an airline hostess for a major airline and had visited many parts of the world. Victor met her after she had got a promotion in the same company and had been assigned to a very good administrative position. Lara was adjusting to her new work and sometimes felt frustrated and even thought about other work opportunities. Victor wanted to "save" her from her frustrations and verbalised his wish to be her saviour. Lara responded and told Victor in very clear terms that she was not a woman in need of saving. She often spent nights with Victor, and one night he woke her up and said: "Let's get out of here". In the past when he had a stable dissociative state he would not remember his conversations, but this time he recalled how Lara told him she had no intention of leaving the room. Victor told his analyst that his relationship with Lara was a reflection of his learning to have a different type of relationship with a woman, something that was new for him. Referring to Lara, he declared: "I am in love for the first time". It was clear that Victor had displaced some of his libidinal transference expectations from his analyst to Lara. He was also having a different relationship with his analyst. Dr. Adeline, too, no longer needed to remain "defective", but Victor would not show any open erotic interest in Dr. Adeline. He brought dreams, instead of describing new actions, to illustrate how he was getting well. In one dream a bus was driven away. "I do not know who drove it away", he said, "I was not in it". In another dream he saw a raven on a roof. The raven watched Victor and then flew away and disappeared. Victor thought that the raven was his SS grandfather's image, and the dream illustrated his freedom from this image.

He no longer saw himself as an Olympic runner, and this materialised again in a reference he made to Lara. In the past Victor bragged about being the man who could best hold an erection for a long time. Now, he easily shared with Dr. Adeline his reaching orgasm one evening as soon as he entered his girlfriend's vagina. He also recalled how Mariel would not tolerate sleeping with him because of his "nightly panic attacks". Lara was so different. She was good to Bernd too and played football with the boy at the weekends. Instead of having a "dissociative state" and breaking a window, Victor checked that the window of the boy's room in his apartment was secure; he wanted to be sure that little boy would not open the window and fall from the third floor.

After he started seeing Dr. Adeline again three times a week, Victor still kept a secret from her for almost a year. It should be recalled that, with financial help from his parents and Mariel's family, he had bought a boarding house and started a rental business. After his separation from

Mariel she had stopped being a partner in this venture. Meanwhile the place needed major renovations and it became very difficult to find tenants. Victor's earnings were disappearing fast, and apparently he was having major financial problems. The boarding house was put on the market, but there were no offers for it. He hid this information from his analyst. Again his main reason was psychological: he could not be a "defective person".

It was a big relief when the boarding house was sold. Then Victor shared the story of his financial difficulties with his analyst. In one of his following sessions he talked about coming clean and not hiding anything from Lara about his financial difficulties. In German "coming clean" is expressed as someone "dropping his or her pants". Dr. Adeline wondered what an observer would see if Victor dropped his pants. Victor replied that the observer would see his "soft and vulnerable" parts. His associations led them discuss his surgery, his defensive habit of having long erections, his hiding his vulnerability since vulnerable people could be gassed, and so on. Dr. Adeline and her patient had a chance to review these issues once more, this time with words and feelings. But Victor was also involved in an action. After reporting that he had soft and vulnerable body parts he started to come to his sessions wearing a cap on his head. Dr. Adeline explained to him that now his head symbolised his penis and wearing the cap was his way of defending it. Victor stopped wearing a cap. He started feeling comfortable being a regular, average guy and once more referred to the idea of terminating his work with Dr. Adeline.

Before describing the termination of his psychoanalysis, I will tell other stories illuminating his working through his problems. One story is about his request to his father to see his grandfather's remaining letters. His father insisted that he had given his son all the "readable letters". He gave his son the same letters again. Victor looked at them once more and did not learn anything new. This event initiated a deep discussion between Victor and Dr. Adeline about the historical truth about the SS grandfather. Victor once more investigated publicly available information about his grandfather. There were hints that even after his grandfather had gone to the Russian front he was involved in the extermination of Jewish people and/or "partisans" involved in various resistance movements.

By this time Lara had moved into his rented apartment and slept with Victor every night in the same bed. Bernd had his own bedroom at weekends. There was much news around this time about a plane crash and passengers missing in the sea. One evening this news was day residue for Victor who saw a hole next to the bed he was sharing with Lara, and an old man and woman and a child vanished into this hole. He was not sure if this was a dream or if he imagined the hole, the old woman, old man, and the child. Dr. Adeline and Victor recalled *The Tell-Tale Heart* and talked about Victor's wish and attempts to separate from the images of his grandfather and his family's story. Then Victor was astonished when Bernd came to his and Lara's bedroom and told him that there was a hole in the floor exactly where Victor had imagined or dreamt seeing one. Bernd also imagined that firefighters went through this hole and put out a fire. This event fascinated Victor. He had no idea of the role he might have played in little Bernd's fantasy, but it made him a true believer in transgenerational transmission. Victor then went to his parents' home and told them about his dream of the hole and how Bernd imagined seeing a hole in the same place. He explained to the old couple that because transgenerational transmissions had made an impact on his son, he had to insist on seeing *all* his grandfather's letters. The father supposedly let him have all the letters and he took them to his apartment. He could not look at them right away, but when he felt ready he read them. Once more there was no new drastic information about his grandfather in them. Personally, I wondered if the father had got rid of any material that contained a hint of the SS officer's criminal behaviour. In any case, after reading all of his grandfather's letters and returning them to his father, Victor's relationship with his father changed. Victor found himself thinking of his father as a small child, how lonely and confused he might have been. Soon after this he visited his father and they built a birdhouse together, the first time in his life he had spent time with the older man without anyone else around. Victor told Dr. Adeline that after that he did not experience tension when visiting his father's house.

I did not hear from Dr. Adeline for months, until she let me know that Lara was pregnant. At that time Bernd was almost three years old. During his sessions Victor compared Mariel's pregnancy with Lara's and began fixing up another room in the huge apartment for his second child. He planned to marry Lara and terminate his analysis. This time Dr. Adeline agreed that her work with Victor had come to an end. Victor married Lara before finishing his analysis.

CHAPTER TWELVE

Another look at identification, depositing, and transgenerational transmission

In Chapter One I referred to a Jewish man who was Dr. Ira Brenner's patient. He described how this man did something illegal and because of it he was jailed at the very age that his father had been during his hiding and escape from, and subsequent capture by, the Gestapo. This man's action that got him jailed was his expression of identification with his father. I do not know if he had other psychological motivations for his behaviour, and I have no information about the nature of his entanglement with the law that sent him to jail, but Dr. Brenner's patient's story reminded me of the story of a German man who came to analysis. I was an occasional consultant for this German individual's analyst, also a German. Let us call this patient Fritz. I will never forget what Fritz did at age forty-nine that forced the authorities to admit him to a mental institution with the threat that he would end up in jail if he did not receive psychotherapeutic help. This was his reason for seeing an analyst. Fritz's bizarre behaviour that got him into this situation started with his writing a letter to his wife, using obscene language and calling her a whore. In the letter he openly described his sexual activities with his wife and her lack of response to his special sexual demands. He made three hundred copies of this letter and distributed them personally to all mailboxes in the district of town where he and his wife lived, along with a photo of his "dishonoured" wife. When Fritz came to treatment he acknowledged that he might be imprisoned for writing and distributing the letters, but he believed that dishonouring his wife was the correct punishment for her "crimes" of not keeping her "promise" to acquiesce to her husband's special sexual demands and her accessing his secret bank accounts in order to secure funds for herself. Fritz was required to stay in analysis until it was terminated or face serving jail time.

The mental representation of Fritz's father's membership in the Waffen-SS (Armed Protective Squadron), a paramilitary organisation within the SS, and the ideology of the SS, appeared in Fritz's internalised object relations and interpersonal interactions, and was a factor in his becoming a malignant letter writer. I will compare Fritz's identification with his father with Victor's being a reservoir of his SS grandfather's mental representation.

Fritz's father, a car mechanic, did not fulfill the requirements to become an official member of the SS because he was not tall enough and had no aristocratic background. However, because he was a good mechanic he was drafted by the SS when World War II began and eventually became a *Hauptsturmführer*, a rather high-level officer commanding four hundred people. He was responsible for the technical maintenance and repair of weapons, trucks, and tanks for a division of several thousand people. It is not known whether Fritz's father ever worked in a concentration camp, but his analyst learned that he had access to Dachau. For example, he once organised prisoners from Dachau to repair bomb damage in a certain section of the town where he lived with his wife and three daughters. At that time Fritz was not yet born. Along with his military rank, this gave his family a high social status.

After the war was over Fritz's father was sentenced to three years in an American punishment camp—interestingly enough he was sent to Dachau to serve his prison term. After he came back home in 1947, his son Fritz was born. While his son was growing up, his father continued to state that he was punished simply for being a member of the military elite unit, the Waffen-SS; but it is more probable that he had committed war crimes. Fritz's father also continued to refer to Dachau as "the hunger camp", referring more to a psychological hunger than the physical one when he was there. As a former SS officer, he was severely humiliated by being placed with men of lower rank and forced to share common public toilets with people who would have been his underlings during the Nazi regime.

When Fritz's father was serving his sentence there was a complete social and economic breakdown of his family. Their property was taken away and Fritz's mother, who used to enjoy the local mayor's and other big shots' company during the Nazi days, had to provide for herself and three daughters by scavenging in trash cans. When Fritz's father returned home, his pre-war character had changed dramatically. During his son's treatment his analyst and I came to the following conclusions: Fritz's father originally felt humiliated since he had thought that, because of his height, he would not be accepted as a member of the SS. After he became a member of the Waffen-SS he used his position to defend against "inferiority". Being sentenced to a punishment camp forced him into a degraded, inferior position and he felt humiliated again. Upon returning home, he externalised his humiliated, traumatised self on to his family by degrading and terrorising them. He defensively over-identified with the SS in order to compensate for his shortcomings. For him the safest place to turn into a symbolic concentration camp was his home, where he could remain in command. Sometimes at four in the morning he would scream at his family and demand that they all appear for roll call. It should be remembered that roll calls (*Appellplatz*) were daily events in the Nazi concentration camps. He rationed the money his wife could spend each day, one Deutsche Mark. His wife and children remained perpetually hungry. He was involved in a process, what Harold Searles (1965) would call, "driving the other crazy", in his case his wife, in order to defend against his own mental breakdown. For example, he would give his wife choices for killing herself: by hanging, drowning, or electrocution. He would call her a "whore" and take her sense of honour away. He would beat her, and later he raped one of his daughters.

It is not my aim in this book to go into details about Fritz's developmental years and incredible childhood traumas, but in general it is clear that Fritz was born into a murderous and chaotic atmosphere after his father's return from the punishment camp. Briefly, his mother was in mental hospitals on and off, and in her delusional states she communicated with Hitler's "depressed sister" and imagined herself married to Stalin. Fritz's older sisters took care of him. In the kindergarten he experienced separation-individuation (Mahler, 1968) problems, crying spells, and spider and rat phobias. He was also concerned about encounters with the image of a black dog. It should be recalled that SS uniforms were all black. His imagined encounters with the black dog image most likely represented his attempts to identify with the aggressor. As he was growing up, Fritz grasped on to identification with his father, an aggressor, for solutions for his internal problems: primarily to be saved from the impact of not having experiences with a good-enough mother and experiencing serious traumas while mentally developing. He was involved in activities that illustrate his identification with his father and the SS. Fritz spent much time creating battles with toy soldiers, bringing the dead ones back to life and killing them again until the final survivors were identified; ultimately these last survivors were the ones whom he considered the losers. To understand one aspect of this paradoxical thought, we need to consider not only what happened to his father (as a survivor he was punished), but also how he described the fate of the SS to his son.

Casualties among the Waffen-SS during the war were very high. The estimated life span at the Russian front was about one and a half years. So, on one level, members of the Waffen-SS might be concerned about whether they would be dead or alive at the end of the war. But SS ethics demanded and instilled in them that the highest achievement was to be ready to give one's life for Hitler. Fritz's father had a handwritten letter from the SS acknowledging him as a master car mechanic, and the stationery is bordered with the motto of readiness to give one's life for the Führer. Fritz believed that this rare handwritten document made his father very proud. It made him feel that he belonged to the elite, despite his shortcomings. To be an elite, however, was to die or to be punished.

In a sense Fritz's father never left the SS. He belonged to *Hilfsgemeinschaft auf Gegenseitigkeit der Angehörigen der ehemaligen Waffen-SS* (HIAG), an organisation of former SS members formed in 1951 for mutual assistance and support. Since there was a social stigma attached to the former SS in post-war Germany, this organisation was founded so that former SS members could help each other. Fritz's father freely talked in front of his son about his life in the SS. For example, he would openly describe how being an SS officer had made women offer him sex; he also talked about having sexual affairs when he was married.

When Fritz was fourteen years old his mother once more entered a mental hospital, this time for decades, until she died there. Fritz became more involved with his father, who had divorced Fritz's mother. The older man had a garage; young Fritz began working there, and received his own professional mechanic's training. After his military service Fritz married his first wife, whom he knew from kindergarten, had two children with her, and continued to work at his father's garage. He followed his father's model of having multiple extramarital affairs. The two men talked openly about their similar behaviour patterns. Fritz was divorced after thirteen years of marriage, in the same year his father died. During his analysis he recalled the last day of his father's life, how his father for the first time touched Fritz's face affectionately and called him "my boy", and how Fritz felt "emotionally close" to his father. His father had chosen music by Wagner to be played at his funeral. Upon hearing the music during the funeral, Fritz felt that his father had at last gone "home". It was understood that his mourning process over his father increased and solidified his identification with the lost object, the aggressor SS father.

Three years later his mother also died and Fritz married again. Just as his father was drastically changed after he was imprisoned and came back home, Fritz's personality also drastically changed after his second marriage. He felt that part of him was living in a "granite tower" that had to be hidden from the public while he tried to act like a regular husband. But he knew that he had picked someone in the community, his second wife, to be the "inferior" one. As years passed he was aware that he wanted to be "his majesty" at home and play "master and slave" games with his wife. In the tenth year of his marriage his wife kicked him out of the house when she found a list of prostitutes in his pocket. Six months after leaving home, Fritz wrote the letter I described above and went from mailbox to mailbox distributing copies of it. During his treatment he described how he was aware of making the humiliation of his wife a community affair, like Nazis (SS) who publicly shamed Jews by forcing them to wear a yellow star or clean the streets with toothbrushes. His fantasy was that when he saw his wife after the letter had been distributed, he would see the face of a person living in terror, like Jews, who were outcasts, fearing for their lives. His father was a member of the SS for about ten years before he was punished by the Americans. After ten years of marriage to his second wife, in a sense Fritz himself ended his SS career: he committed a crime based upon the SS model and expected to be punished as his father had been punished. His treatment did not help Fritz much. He developed severe chronic infection in his ears which produced stinking pus. He died on the day before a court would decide on his divorce procedure.

The main difference between the occurrence of transgenerational transmission of Nazi-related behaviour patterns in Fritz's and Victor's cases is that Fritz knew and interacted with his father while Victor was born long after his grandfather's death. Fritz's father openly talked about his life during the Nazi regime while Victor's parents kept silent about his grandfather's role in the Third Reich. In Fritz's case we can see the role of identification and in Victor's case the role of depositing in transgenerational transmission; both of them, one of the second and the other of the third generation, had remained carriers of the impact of historical events.

Both identification and depositing processes take place silently. An examiner cannot put her finger on the moment when an identification or depositing takes place and becomes solidified. Observing children or hearing patients' childhood stories during their analyses provide examples of how these processes slowly proceed. Fritz's obsession with toy soldiers and the specific nature of his play with them was an example of his identification with his SS father. Fritz was the *active* partner in absorbing his father's image and associated psychological tasks that were related to Third Reich history.

The best way to observe an identification process that happens in adulthood is to work with individuals in grief and mourning following the loss of a person who is psychologically important to them. Freud's (1917) "Mourning and melancholia" is the first paper that deals with internalised object relations of an adult mourner. Adult-type mourning can be divided into two phases: (1) the grief reaction, and (2) the work of mourning. The grief reaction includes responses such as shock, denial, and bargaining to reverse the outcome, pain, and anger, all of which, especially anger, eventually lead to the beginning of an emotional "knowledge" that the lost object is gone. In a typical situation, anger is not directed towards a loved one who has died. This would not be acceptable to a "normal" superego. The mourner becomes angry at the physician who did not take good care of the loved one or the cold weather that began the loved one's illness. Before grief is completed, the work of mourning, as Freud described, begins. This phase of mourning involves a slow process of revisiting, reviewing, and transforming the mourner's emotional investment in the images of the lost object. The work of mourning refers to an internal encounter between the images of the lost object and the corresponding self-images of the mourner. Since unassimilated mental images of lost objects remain in our psyche even when they are tamed, shrunk, repressed, or denied, adult-type mourning in a sense never ends until the mourner dies (Kernberg, 2010;

Volkan & Zintl, 1993). The completion of a "normal" mourning process means, as Veikko Tähkä (1984, 1993) stated, that the mourner makes the mental representation of the lost person or thing "futureless". However, even the mental representation of the lost person, which for all practical purposes had been rendered "futureless", may become active again, such as during anniversaries of important relationships with the person prior to the physical disappearance.

Sometimes in our clinical practice we see individuals who provide us illustrations of an internalised mental representation of the lost person that is not yet assimilated into its carrier's self-representation. Such an observation clearly shows how we "take in" another person's mental representation, or at least some of that person's special images. A new patient of mine complained that while driving to work in his car his brother constantly talked with him, even when my patient wanted some time for himself or when he wanted to listen to the car radio. His brother made suggestions as to how my patient should behave when meeting his boss or when talking to a particular secretary at work. Sometimes my patient told his brother to shut up, but the younger man continued to talk and irritate him. In my mind, I pictured my patient in his car with his brother sitting next to him. Therefore, I was completely surprised when my patient, in his sixth therapeutic session, informed me that his younger brother had died six years earlier in an accident. The "brother" with whom he had conversations while driving to work was actually his brother's unassimilated object representation (Volkan, 2007).

A good example of identification was provided by a philandering young man. A year or so after his father's death he became a serious industrialist, as his dead father had been. I had met his father, and I remembered that he had a habit of touching his hair in a special way when talking about a serious matter. Now his son was exhibiting the same gesture. Identifications can be "healthy" or "unhealthy" according to the clinician's judgment. I can say that Fritz's identification with his father's mental representation was an "unhealthy" one. It increased and became more solidified following the loss of his father. I imagine that the "granite tower" that he sensed within himself stood as a symbolic representation of his father's Waffen-SS mental image; he treated his wife as if she was a Jewish person at the mercy of a Nazi, just as his father had done when relating to Fritz's mother.

Victor was the *passive* partner in the process of internalising his grandfather's mental representation, which was a "made-up" representation in the minds of his parents, especially his father. When this "made-up" object representation was deposited into Victor it was too confusing to be fully assimilated; it had different parts that could not meld together. The sadistic historical image of the grandfather, also originally in the minds of parents, was placed into little Victor's mind, scaring him. The other part of the "made up" mental representation was the "Saviour" or the "Firefighter" whose main task was to reverse horrible deeds associated with the first image and remove shame and guilt feelings. The "made-up" mental representation also had to be grandiose, and it kept alive the inflated self-esteem and the entitlement of a big shot Nazi SS officer. Because what was deposited in Victor was so confusing, he could not develop an integrated self-representation. During his daily life his dissociated self was "locked" away. His dissociated self contained images of grandfather with aggression and sadism, as well as the corresponding self-image of the fighter against dangers due to grandfather's aggression and sadism. Victor's overt self-representation also included his grandfather's "superior", entitled aspects. He also had to manage to feel "well" and help others to feel "well" and even be the "best" in this or that in order not to attract the attention of any Nazi involved in the killing of "disabled" persons. He tried not to contaminate his overt self-representation with open aggression and sadism.

The previous chapters outline how Victor's parents created an atmosphere in which there existed a "defective" child facing death and the necessity of keeping an omnipotent "saviour". I do not know when Victor actually heard or read about the T4 euthanasia programme without consciously associating it with his grandfather's position as an SS officer. Living in Germany, sooner or later, he would have learned about such historical events. But as a small child he did not have this information; his parents had this knowledge. Victor's parents behaved in their daily lives as if the T4 programme still existed, but had to be kept a secret. Victor's father's prestigious job as an administrator of a private university was the extra, and realistic, reason that he and his wife kept this secret.

Many years after starting to work with Dr. Adeline Victor realised how his father re-enacted the influence of the euthanasia programme in his hobby of raising geraniums in flower pots. Anything "unwanted", such as a dead or even crooked leaf, had to be removed from the plants. There should be no "defective" plant. Victor's father, also, was preoccupied with the task of protecting the flowers from rain or being eaten by deer. If he was going away for a day or so, he would carefully wrap a plastic cover over each potted geranium. Only after Victor found out about his grandfather and shared this information with his father, did the older man give up his geranium hobby. After learning about his grandfather's deeds and after the birth of Bernd, the patient also noticed how his father would become anxious and could not tolerate seeing a child cry. Most likely, Victor's father had similar reactions to a child in distress long before adult Victor noticed it. Victor connected his observation of his father's anxiety with the idea of having a "defective child" around who could be put to death and the fear of not being able to save the child.

Differentiating between identification and being subject to depositing is sometimes difficult. One can state that child Victor was active in identifying with his father's behaviour in raising geraniums or avoiding crying children. However, reading his developmental story clearly illustrates that he could not have been the active partner in absorbing images connected with Nazi history. For example, when he was "gassed" during his tonsillectomy as a child he could not connect his traumatic experience with Nazis gassing innocent persons. His parents made this connection. I already suggested that locked letters might be a model for Victor's "locked" (encapsulated) dissociated state. We can add to the psychological significance of locked-up letters the psychological significance of geranium pots wrapped in plastic protectors and, of course, his parents' decades-long silence and his mother saying to her son that if the silence was broken the son would expose them to a "trial".

Of course, the influence of images of historical events, which are settled within an individual due to identifications or being a reservoir of depositing, or both, become intertwined with this individual's other internal elements. Such elements in each person are different from those belonging to another, due to the influence of factors ranging from constitutional biological ones, to family environment, to the types of traumas that are not connected with shared historical events, to the nature of unconscious fantasies that develop in childhood.

In summarising Fritz's case in this last chapter I illustrate that persons like him and like Victor, who are innocent, sometimes suffer greatly or also cause suffering to other innocent persons, simply because they are descendants of perpetrators involved in tragic, shared societal traumas.

REFERENCES

Abse, D. W. (1983). Multiple personality. In: S. Akhtar (Ed.), *New Psychiatric Syndromes: DSM–III and Beyond* (pp. 339–361). New York: Jason Aronson.

Ainslie, R. C. & Solyom, A. E. (1986). The replacement of fantastical oedipal child: A disruptive effect of sibling loss on the mother-infant relationship. *Psychoanalytic Psychology*, 3: 257–268.

Akhtar, S. (1999). *Immigration and Identity: Turmoil, Treatment and Transformation*. London: Karnac.

Akhtar, S. (2009). *Comprehensive Dictionary of Psychoanalysis*. London: Karnac.

Akhtar, S. & Thomson, J. A. (1982). Overview: Narcissistic personality disorder. *American Journal of Psychiatry*, 139: 12–20.

Alderdice, J. (2007). The individual, the group and the psychology of terrorism. *International Review of Psychiatry*, 19: 201–209.

Alderdice, J. (2010). Off the couch and round the conference table. In: A. Lemma & M. Patrick (Eds.), *Contemporary Psychoanalytic Applications* (pp. 15–32). New York & London: Routledge.

Apprey, M. (1993). The African-American experience: Forced immigration and transgenerational trauma. *Mind and Human Interaction*, 4: 70–75.

Apprey, M. (1998). Reinventing the self in the face of received transgenerational hatred in the African American community. *Mind and Human Interaction*, 9: 30–37.

Arlow, J. A. (1973). Motivations for peace. In: H. Z. Winnik, R. Moses, & M. Ostow (Eds.), *Psychological Basis of War* (pp. 193–204). Jerusalem: Jerusalem Academic Press.

Ast, G. (1991). Interviews with Germans about reunification. *Mind and Human Interaction*, 2: 100–104.

Bach, S. (2006). *Getting from Here to There*. Hillsdale, NJ: Analytic Press.

Blum, H. P. (1976). Acting out, the psychoanalytic process, and interpretation. *Annual of Psychoanalysis*, 4: 163–184.

Blum, H. P. (1985). Superego formation, adolescent transformation and the adult neurosis. *Journal of the American Psychoanalytic Association*, 4: 887–909.

Boccara, B. (2014). *Socio-Analytic Dialogue: Incorporating Psychosocial Dynamics into Public Policies*. New York: Lexington Press.

Brenner, I. (1994). The dissociative character: A reconsideration of "multiple personality". *Journal of the American Psychoanalytic Association*, 42: 819–846.

Brenner, I. (2001). *Dissociation of Trauma: Theory, Phenomenology, and Technique*. Madison, CT: International Universities Press.

Brenner, I. (2002). Foreword. In: V. D. Volkan, G. Ast, & W. Greer, *The Third Reich in the Unconscious: Transgenerational Transmission and its Consequences* (pp. xi–xvii). New York: Brunner-Routledge.

Brenner, I. (2004). *Psychic Trauma: Dynamics, Symptoms, and Treatment*. New York: Jason Aronson.

Brenner, I. (2014). *Dark Matters: Exploring the Realm of Psychic Devastation*. London: Karnac.

Brenner, I. (2015). Personal communication.

Cain, A. C. & Cain, B. S. (1964). On replacing a child. *Journal of the American Academy of Child Psychiatry*, 3: 443–456.

Cameron, N. (1961). Introjection, reprojection, and hallucination in the interaction between schizophrenic patient and therapist. *International Journal of Psychoanalysis*, 42: 86–96.

Cooper, A. M. (1989). Narcissism and masochism: The narcissistic-masochistic character. *Psychiatric Clinics of North America*, 12: 541–552.

Dorpat, T. L. (2002). *Wounded Monster: Hitler's Path from Trauma to Malevolence*. New York: University Press of America.

Eckstaedt, A. (1989). *Nationalsozialismus in der "zweiten Generation": Psychoanalyse von Hörigkeitsverhältnissen (National Socialism in the Second Generation: Psychoanalysis of Master-Slave Relationships)*. Frankfurt A. M.: Suhrkamp Verlag.

Ekstein, R. N. (1966). *Children of Time and Space, of Action and Impulse: Clinical Studies on the Psychoanalytic Treatment of Severely Disturbed Children*. East Norwalk, CT: Appleton-Century Crofts.

Elliott, M., Bishop, K. & Stokes, P. (2004). Societal PTSD? Historic shock in Northern Ireland. *Psychotherapy and Politics International*, 2: 1–16.

Erikson, E. H. (1956). The problem of ego identity. *Journal of the American Psychoanalytic Association*, 4: 56–121.

Erlich, H. S. (2010). A beam of darkness—understanding the terrorist mind. In: H. Brunning & M. Perini (Eds.), *Psychoanalytic Perspectives on a Turbulent World* (pp. 3–15). London: Karnac.

Faimberg, H. (2005). *The Telescoping of Generations: Listening to the Narcissistic Links Between Generations*. London: Routledge.

Falzeder, E. & Brabant, E. (2000). *The Correspondence of Sigmund Freud and Sándor Ferenczi, 3*: 1920–1933, P. Hoffer (Trans.). Cambridge, MA: Harvard University Press.

Fenichel, O. (1945). *The Psychoanalytic Theory of Neurosis*. New York: W. W. Norton.

Fornari, F. (1966). *The Psychoanalysis of War*. A. Pfeifer (Trans.). Bloomington: Indiana University Press, 1975.

Freud, S. (1900). The Interpretation of Dreams. *S. E.*, 4 & 5. London: Hogarth.

Freud, S. (1905). Three Essays on the Theory of Sexuality. *S. E.*, 7: 123–243. London: Hogarth.

Freud, S. (1914). Remembering, repeating and working-through. *S. E.*, 12: 147–156. London: Hogarth.

Freud, S. (1917). Mourning and melancholia. *S. E.*, 14: 237–258. London: Hogarth.

Freud, S. (1920). Beyond the Pleasure Principle. *S. E.*, 18: 7–64. London: Hogarth.

Freud, S. (1925). An autobiographical study. *S. E.*, 20: 7–70. London: Hogarth.

Freud, S. (1932). Why War? *S. E.*, 22: 197–215. London: Hogarth.

Friedman, P. (1949). Some aspects of concentration camp psychology. *American Journal of Psychiatry*, 105: 601–605.

Fromm, G. (2011). *Lost in Transmission: Studies of Trauma Across Generations*. London: Karnac.

Gilbert, M. (2006). *Kristallnacht: Prelude to Destruction*. New York: HarperCollins.

Giovacchini, P. L. (1969). The influence of interpretation upon schizophrenic patients. *International Journal of Psychoanalysis*, 50: 179–186.

Giovacchini, P. L. (1972). Interpretation and the definition of the analytic setting. In: P. L. Giovacchini (Ed.), *Tactics and Techniques in Psychoanalytic Therapy, Vol. II* (pp. 5–94). New York: Jason Aronson.

Glower, E. (1947). *War, Sadism, and Pacifism: Further Essays on Group Psychology and War*. London: Allen & Unwin.

Gobodo-Madikizela, P. G. & Van der Merwe, C. (2009). *Memory, Narrative and Forgiveness: Perspectives on the Unfinished Journeys of the Past*. Newcastle upon Tyne, UK: Cambridge Scholars.

Grayling, A. C. (2006). *Among the Dead Cities*. London: Bloomsbury.

Green, N. & Solnit, A. J. (1964). Reactions to the threatened loss of a child: A vulnerable child syndrome. *Pediatrics, 34*: 58–66.

Grubrich-Simitis, I. (1979). Extremtraumatisierung als kumulatives Trauma: Psychoanalytische Studien über seelische Nachwirkungen der Konzentrationslagerhaft bei Űberlebenden und ihren Kindern (Extreme traumatization as a cumulative trauma: Psychoanalytic studies on the mental effects of imprisonment in concentration camps on survivors and their children). *Psyche, 33*: 991–1023.

Hartmann, H. (1939). *Ego Psychology and the Problem of Adaptation*. New York: International Universities Press.

Hartmann, H. (1951). Technical Implication of ego psychology. *Psychoanalytic Quarterly, 20*: 31–43.

Hollander, N. (1997). *Love in a Time of Hate: Liberation Psychology in Latin America*. New York: Other Press.

Hollander, N. (2010). *Uprooted Minds: Surviving the Political Terror in the Americas*. New York: Taylor & Francis.

Jokl, A. M. (1997). *Zwei Fälle zum Thema "Bewältigung der Vergangenheit"* (Two Cases Referring to the Theme of "Mastering the Past"). Frankfurt A. M.: Jüdischer Verlag.

Kakar, S. (1996). *The Colors of Violence: Cultural Identities, Religion, and Conflict*. Chicago: University of Chicago Press.

Kernberg, O. F. (1970). Factors in the psychoanalytic treatment of narcissistic personalities. *Journal of the American Psychoanalytic Association, 18*: 51–85.

Kernberg, O. F. (1975). *Borderline Conditions and Pathological Narcissism*. New York: Jason Aronson.

Kernberg, O. F. (2010). Some observations on the process of mourning. *International Journal of Psychoanalysis, 91*: 601–619.

Kestenberg, J. S. (1982). A psychological assessment based on analysis of a survivor's child. In: M. S. Bergman & M. E. Jucovy (Eds.), *Generations of the Holocaust* (pp. 158–177). New York: Columbia University Press.

Klein, M. (1946). Notes on some schizoid mechanisms. *International Journal of Psychoanalysis, 27*: 99–110.

Klein, M. (1961). *Narrative of a Child Analysis: The Conduct of the Psychoanalysis of Children as Seen in the Treatment of a Ten-Year-Old Boy*. London: Hogarth, 1975.

Kluft, R. P. (1993). Clinical approaches to the integration of personalities. In: R. P. Kluft & C. G. Fine (Eds.), *Clinical Perspectives on Multiple Personality Disorder* (pp. 101–134). Washington, DC: American Psychiatric Press.

Kogan, I. (2007). *The Struggle Against Mourning*. New York: Jason Aronson.
Kohut, H. (1966). Forms and transformations of narcissism. *Journal of the American Psychoanalytic Association*, 14: 243–272.
Kohut, H. (1971). *The Analysis of the Self: A Systematic Approach to the Psychoanalytic Treatment of Narcissistic Personality Disorders*. New York: International Universities Press.
Krystal, H. (Ed.) (1968). *Massive Psychic Trauma*. New York: International Universities Press.
Kuriloff, E. A. (2013). *Contemporary Psychoanalysis and the Legacy of the Third Reich: History, Memory, Tradition*. New York: Routledge.
Langer, W. C. (1972). *The Mind of Hitler: The Secret Wartime Report*. New York: Basic.
Laub, D. & Auerhahn, N. C. (1993). Knowing and not knowing psychic trauma: Forms of traumatic memory. *International Journal of Psychoanalysis*, 74: 287–302.
Laub, D. & Podell, D. (1995). Art and trauma. *International Journal of Psychoanalysis*, 76: 871–1081.
Legg, C. & Sherick, I. (1976). The replacement child–A developmental tragedy: Some preliminary comments. *Child Psychiatry and Human Development*, 7: 79–97.
Lifton, R. J. (1968). *Death in Life: Survivors of Hiroshima*. New York: Random House.
Lifton, R. J. (1986). *The Nazi Doctors: Medical Killing and the Psychology of Genocide*. New York: Basic.
Loewald, H. W. (1960). On the therapeutic action of psychoanalysis. *International Journal of Psychoanalysis*, 41: 16–33.
Loewenberg, P. (1991). Uses of anxiety. *Partisan Review*, 3: 514–525.
Loewenstein, R. M. (1951). The problem of interpretation. *The Psychoanalytic Quarterly*, 20: 1–14.
Loewenstein, R. M. (1958). Remarks on some variations in psychoanalytic technique. *International Journal of Psychoanalysis*, 39: 202–210.
Maaz, H.-J. (1991). *Das Gestürzte Volk* [The Fallen People]. Berlin: Argon Verlag.
Mahler, M. S. (1968). *On Human Symbiosis and the Vicissitudes of Individuation*. New York: International Universities Press.
Misselwitz, I. (2003). German reunification: A quasi ethnic conflict. *Mind and Human Interaction*, 13: 77–86.
Mitscherlich, A. (1971). Psychoanalysis and aggression of large groups. *International Journal of Psychoanalysis*, 52: 161–167.
Mitscherlich, A. & Mitscherlich, M. (1975). *The Inability to Mourn: Principals of Collective Behavior*. B. R. Placzek (Trans.). New York: Grove, 1967.
Modell, A. H. (1975). A narcissistic defense against affects and the illusion of self-sufficiency. *International Journal of Psychoanalysis*, 56: 275–282.

Moore, B. E. & Fine, B. D. (1990). *Psychoanalytic Terms and Concepts*. New Haven, CT: The American Psychoanalytic Association and Yale University Press.
Moses, R. (1984). An Israeli psychologist looks back in 1983. In: S. A. Luel & P. Marcus (Eds.), *Psychoanalytic Reflections on the Holocaust: Selected Essays* (pp. 52–70). New York: Ktav Publishing House.
Moses, R. (Ed.) (1993). *Persistent Shadows of the Holocaust: The Meaning to Those Not Directly Affected*. Madison, CT: International Universities Press.
Niederland, W. (1961). The problem of the survivor. *Journal of the Hillside Hospital, 10*: 233–247.
Niederland, W. (1968). Clinical observations on the "survivor syndrome". *International Journal of Psychoanalysis, 49*: 313–315.
Novey, S. (1968). *The Second Look: The Reconstruction of Personal History in Psychiatry and Psychoanalysis*. Baltimore: Johns Hopkins Press.
Ohlmeier, D. (1991). The return of the repressed: Psychoanalytical reflections on the unification of Germany. Paper presented to the Sandor Ferenczi Society, Budapest, 7 June.
Opher-Cohn, L., Pfäfflin, J., Sonntag, J. B., Klose, B., & Pogany-Wnendt, P. (Eds.) (2000). *Das Ende der Sprachlosigkeit? Auswirkungen traumatischer Holocausterfahrungen über mehrere Generationen* [End of Speechlesnes? The Effects of Experiencing the Holocaust over Several Generations]. Gießen: Psychosozial Verlag.
Ornstein, A. (2004). *My Mother's Eyes: Holocaust Memories of a Young Girl*. Covington, KY: Clerisy Press.
Paláez, M. G. (2009). Trauma theory in Sándor Ferenczi's writings, 1931–1932. *International Journal of Psychoanalysis, 90*: 1217–1233.
Parens, H. (2004). *Renewal of Life: Healing From the Holocaust*. Rockville, MD: Schriber.
Poland, W. S. (1977). Pilgrimage: Action and tradition in self-analysis. *Journal of the American Psychoanalytic Association, 25*: 399–416.
Poznanski, E. O. (1972). The "replacement child": A saga of unresolved parental grief. *Behavioral Pediatrics, 81*: 1190–1193.
Proctor, R. (1988). *Racial Hygiene: Medicine Under the Nazis*. Boston, MA: Harvard University Press.
Rachman, A. W. (1997). The suppression and censorship of Ferenczi's "Confusion of Tongues" paper. *Psychoanalytic Inquiry, 17*: 459–485.
Rangell, L. (1968). A point of view on acting out. *International Journal of Psychoanalysis, 49*: 195–201.
Rangell, L. (2003). Affects: In an individual and a nation. First Annual Volkan Lecture, 15 November, University of Virginia, Charlottesville, VA.

Rapaport, D. (1951). *Organization and Pathology of Thought: Selected Papers*. New York: Columbia University Press.
Read, A. (1989). *Kristallnacht: The Nazi Night of Terror*. New York: Times Books.
Redlich, F. (1998). *Hitler: Diagnosis of a Destructive Prophet*. New York: Oxford University Press.
Rosenfeld, D. (1992). *The Psychotic: Aspects of the Personality*. London: Karnac.
Rosenfeld, H. A. (1965). *Psychotic States: A Psychoanalytic Approach*. London: Hogarth.
Schützenberger, A. A. (1998). *The Ancestor Syndrome: Transgenerational Psychotherapy and the Hidden Links in the Family Tree*. New York: Routledge.
Searles, H. F. (1965). *Collected Papers on Schizophrenia and Related Subjects*. New York: International Universities Press.
Šebek, M. (1992). Anality in the totalitarian system and the psychology of post-totalitarian society. *Mind and Human Interaction*, 4: 52–59.
Šebek, M. (1994). Psychopathology of everyday life in the post-totalitarian society. *Mind and Human Interaction*, 5: 104–109.
Sonnenberg, S. M. (1974). Children of survivors. *Journal of the American Psychoanalytic Association*, 22: 200–204.
Steinweis, A. E. (2009). *Kristallnacht 1938*. Cambridge, MA: Belknap.
Stern, D. N. (1985). *The Interpersonal World of the Infant*. New York: Basic.
Stern, J. (2001). Deviance in the Nazi society. *Mind and Human Interaction*, 12: 18–237.
Stone, M. H. (1989). Murder. *Psychiatric Clinics of North America*, 12: 643–651.
Streeck-Fischer, A. (1999). Naziskins in Germany: How traumatization deals with the past. *Mind and Human Interaction*, 10: 84–97.
Tähkä, V. (1984). Dealing with object loss. *Scandinavian Psychoanalytic Review*, 7: 13–33.
Tähkä, V. (1993). *Mind and Its Treatment: A Psychoanalytic Approach*. Madison, CT: International Universities Press.
Varvin, S. & Volkan, V. D. (Eds.) (2003). *Violence or Dialogue: Psychoanalytic Insights on Terror and Terrorism*. London: International Psychoanalytical Association.
Volkan, V. D. (1972). The "linking objects" of pathological mourners. *Archives of General Psychiatry*, 27: 215–222.
Volkan, V. D. (1973). Transitional fantasies in the analysis of a narcissistic personality. *Journal of the American Psychoanalytic Association*, 21: 351–376.
Volkan, V. D. (1976). *Primitive Internalized Object Relations: A Clinical Study of Schizophrenic, Borderline and Narcissistic Patients*. New York: International Universities Press.

Volkan, V. D. (1979). The glass bubble of a narcissistic patient. In: J. LeBoit & A. Capponi (Eds.), *Advances in Psychotherapy of the Borderline Patient* (pp. 405–431). New York: Jason Aronson.

Volkan, V. D. (1981). *Linking Objects and Linking Phenomena: A Study of the Forms, Symptoms, Metapsychology, and Therapy of Complicated Mourning*. New York: International Universities Press.

Volkan, V. D. (1982). Narcissistic personality disorder. In: O. Canevar, Jr. & H. K. Brodie (Eds.), *Critical Problems in Psychiatry* (pp. 332–350). Philadelphia, PA: Lippincott.

Volkan, V. D. (1987). *Six Steps in the Treatment of Borderline Personality Organization*. Northvale, NJ: Jason Aronson.

Volkan, V. D. (1988). *The Need to Have Enemies and Allies: From Clinical Practice to International Relationships*. Northvale, NJ: Jason Aronson.

Volkan, V. D. (1990a). The question of Germany: A West German's response. *Mind and Human Interaction*, 1: 2–3, 9.

Volkan, V. D. (1990b). Living statues and political decision making. *Mind and Human Interaction*, 2: 3–4, 19–20.

Volkan, V. D. (1997). *Bloodlines: From Ethnic Pride to Ethnic Terrorism*. New York: Farrar, Straus & Giroux.

Volkan, V. D. (2002). *Kozmik Kahkaha* [Cosmic Laughter]. B. Büyükkal (Trans.). Istanbul: Okuyan Us.

Volkan, V. D. (2003). Large-group identity: Border psychology and related societal processes. *Mind and Human Interaction*, 13: 49–76.

Volkan, V. D. (2004a). *Blind Trust: Large Groups and Their Leaders in Times of Crisis and Terror*. Charlottesville, VA: Pitchstone.

Volkan, V. D. (2004b). Actualized unconscious fantasies and "therapeutic play" in adults' analyses: Further study of these concepts. In: A. Laine (Ed.), *Power of Understanding: Essays in Honour of Veikko Tähkä*, (pp. 119–141). London: Karnac.

Volkan, V. D. (2006a). *Killing in the Name of Identity: A Study of Bloody Conflicts*. Charlottesville, VA: Pitchstone.

Volkan, V. D. (2006b). Grossgruppen und ihre Politischen Führer mit Narzisstischer Persönlichkeitsorganisation. In: O. F. Kernberg & H.-P. Hartmann (Eds.), *Narzißmus: Grundlagen-Störungsbilder–Therapie* (pp. 205–227). Stuttgart: Schattauer.

Volkan, V. D. (2007). Individuals and societies as "perennial mourners": Their linking objects and public memorials. In: B. Wilcock, L. C. Bohm, & R. Curtis (Eds.), *On Death and Dying: Psychoanalysts' Reflections on Finality, Transformations and New Beginnings* (pp. 42–59). Philadelphia: Routledge.

Volkan, V. D. (2008). Some psychoanalytic views on leaders with narcissistic personality organization and their roles in large-group processes. In: R. H. Klein, C. A. Rice, & V. L. Schermer (Eds.), *Leadership in a Changing World: Dynamic Perspectives on Groups and Their Leaders* (pp. 67–89). New York: Lexington.

Volkan, V. D. (2010). *Psychoanalytic Technique Expanded: A Textbook of Psychoanalytic Treatment*. Istanbul: Oa Press.

Volkan, V. D. (2013). *Enemies on the Couch: A Psychopolitical Journey Through War and Peace*. Durham, NC: Pitchstone.

Volkan, V. D. (2014a). Father quest and linking objects: A Story of the American World War II Orphans Network (AWON) and Palestinian Orphans. In: P. Cohen, K. M. Sossin, & R. Ruth (Eds.), *Healing After Parent Loss in Childhood and Adolescence* (pp. 283–300). New York: Rowman & Littlefield.

Volkan, V. D. (2014b). *Psychoanalysis, International Relations, and Diplomacy: A Sourcebook on Large-Group Psychology*. London: Karnac.

Volkan, V. D. (2014c). *Animal Killer: Transmission of War Trauma from One Generation to the Next*. London: Karnac.

Volkan, V. D. (2015). *Would-be Wife Killer: A Clinical Study of Primitive Mental Functions, Actualised Unconscious Fantasies, Satellite States. and Developmental Steps*. London: Karnac.

Volkan, V. D. & Ast, G. (1992). *Eine Borderline-Therapie: Strukturelle und Objektbeziehungskonflikte in der Psychoanalyse der Borderline-Persönlichkeitsorganisation* [One Borderline Therapy: Structural and Object Relations Conflict in the Psychoanalysis of Borderline Personality Organization]. Göttingen: Vandenhoeck & Ruprecht.

Volkan, V. D. & Ast, G. (1994). *Spektrum des Narzißmus: Eine klinische Studie des gesunden Narzißmus, des narzißtisch-masochistischen Charakters, der narzißtischen Persönlichkeitsorganisation, des malignen Narzißmus und des erfolgreichen Narzißmus* [Spectrum of Narcissism: A Clinical Study of Healthy Narcissism, Narcissistic-Masochistic Character, Narcissistic Personality-Organization, Malignant Narcissism, and Successful Narcissism]. Göttingen: Vandenhoeck & Ruprecht.

Volkan, V. D. & Ast, G. (1997). *Siblings in the Unconscious and Psychopathology*. Madison, CT: International Universities Press.

Volkan, V. D. & Ast, G. (2001). Curing Gitta's "leaking body": Actualized unconscious fantasies and therapeutic play. *Journal of Clinical Psychoanalysis, 10*: 567–606.

Volkan, V. D., Ast, G. & Greer, W. F. (2002). *The Third Reich in the Unconscious: Transgenerational Transmission and its Consequences*. New York: Brunner-Routledge.

Volkan, V. D. & Fowler, J. C. (2009). *Searching for the Perfect Woman: The Story of a Complete Psychoanalysis*. New York: Jason Aronson.

Volkan, V. D. & Zintl, E. (1993). *Life After Loss: The Lessons of Grief*. New York: Charles Scribner's Sons.

Waelder, R. (1971). Psychoanalysis and history. In: B. B. Wolman (Ed.), *The Psychoanalytic Interpretation of History* (pp. 3–22). New York: Basic.

Weisberger, A. M. (1995). German Reunification and the Jewish Question. *Mind and Human Interaction*, 6: 9–14.

Werman, D. S. (1984). The premature transference. Paper presented at the American Psychoanalytic Association Meeting, San Diego, California, 16–20 May.

Wheelis, A. (1950). The place of action in personality change. *Psychiatry: Journal for the Study of Interpersonal Processes*, *13*: 135–148.

Winnicott, D. W. (1960). Ego distortion in terms of true and false self. In: *The Maturational Processes and the Facilitating Environment* (pp. 140–152). New York: International Universities Press, 1965.

Winnicott, D. W. (1969). Berlin walls. In: C. Winnicott, R. Shepherd, & M. Davis (Eds.), *D. W. Winnicott: Home is Where We Start From* (pp. 221–227). New York: W.W. Norton, 1986.

INDEX

Abse, D. W. 31
acting out 73–74
Ainslie, R. C. 28
Akhtar, S. 12, 24, 30
Alderdice, J. 12
American Psychoanalytic Association 12
analytic (new) object 75, 85
Ankara Medical School 2, 10
Apprey, M. 12
Arlow, J. A. 10
Ast, G. 2, 4–7, 11, 24–25, 27–28, 75, 78
Auerhahn, N. C. 8
Auschwitz x, 3
Austen Riggs Center 85

Bach, S. 25
Blum, H. P. 8, 74
Berlin Wall 2, 4, 13, 81
Biet Atfal al-Sumud 4

Bishop, K. 12
Boccara, B. 13
Brabant, E. 9
Brandt, W. 5
Brenner, I. 8, 11–12, 30–31, 34, 91
British Climate Change Act 65

Cain, A. C. 28
Cain, A. M. 28
Cameron, N. 75, 78
chosen glory 13
chosen trauma 13
circumcision 35, 45, 66
Cooper, A. M. 25
countertransference viii, 75
Cyprus 2, 6, 10–11
    Cypriot Turk xiv

depositing x–xi, 7, 27–28, 96, 99
dissociation 5, 30
Dorpat, T. L. xv

Eckstaedt, A. 5
Ekstein, R. N. 75
Elliott, M. 12
encapsulation 46, 62
entitlement ideology 13
Erikson, E. H. 26
Erlich, H. S. 12

Faimberg, H. 8
Falzeder, E. 9
Fenichel, O. 73
Fine, B. D. 73
Fonagy, P. xi
Fornari, F. 10
Fowler, J. C. 13, 75
Freud, S. x, 9–10, 36, 73–74, 96
Friedman, P. 6–7
Fromm, G. 12

German Psychoanalytic Society 4
Germany ix, xiv, 1–2, 4–6, 13, 21, 49–50, 65, 71, 94, 98
   East Germany xiii, 2–4, 82
   German reunification 3–4
   West Germany xiv, 2–4, 81
Gilbert, M. 72
Giovacchini, P. L. 36, 75, 78
Glower, E. 10
Gobodo-Madikizela, P. G. 6
grandiose self 24–27, 29, 41, 46
Grayling, A. C. 51
Green, N. 28
Greer, W. F. 5–7, 11, 27, 75
Grubrich-Simitis, I. 5
Gyorgy, G. xi

Hitler, A. xv, 3, 49, 54, 65, 69, 93, 94
Hartmann, H. 58
historical events xiii, 8, 12–13, 96, 98–99
Hitler Youth 46, 51, 64, 72
Hollander, N. 12

Holocaust 1–8, 11–12, 47, 52
   Jewish survivors xi, xv, 6–7
hungry self 25–26, 29, 30

identification xi, 27–28, 91, 94–97, 99
   projective identification 28
International Psychoanalytic Association 4, 12
interpretation 36, 80
   enchiladas interpretation 84–85
   linking interpretation 36
   preparatory interpretation 37
Israel 1, 4, 6–8
Israel Psychoanalytic Society 4

Jokl, A. M. 5
Jurist, E. xi

Kakar, S. 12
Kernberg, O. F. 24–25, 75, 78, 96
Kestenberg, J. S. 7, 11
Kristallnacht 72
Klein, M. x, 10, 28, 41
Klose, B. 6
Kluft, R. P. 31
Kogan, I. 8
Kohut, H. 24
Krystal, H. 7
Kuriloff, E. A. x–xi, 8

Langer, W. C. xv
Laub, D. 8
Legg, R. 28
Lifton, R. J. 7, 50
Loewald, H. W. 75, 78
Loewenberg, P. 8
Loewenstein, R. M. 37

Maaz, H.-J. 4
magical thinking 13
Mahler, M. S. 23, 93

Misselwitz, I. 4
Mitscherlich, A. 10
Mitscherlich, M. 10
Modell, A. H. 26, 28
Moore, B. E. 73
Moses, R. 1, 8
mourning 1, 8, 11, 13, 29, 39–40, 46,
    61, 78, 82, 95–97
multiple personality organization 30–31

narcissistic personality organization
    24–31
Nazi ix, xi, xii, xv, 3–7, 46, 49–51,
    53–55, 63–64, 71–73, 79–80,
    83, 92–93, 95–99
Niederland, W. 7
Novey, S. 74
Nuremberg War Tribunal 50, 52, 69

Ohlmeier, D. 4
Opher-Cohn, L. 4–6
Ornstein, A. 8

PAKH 5–6, 11, 13
Paláez, M. G. 9
Parens, H. 8
Pfäfflin, J. 6
pilgrimage 74
Pogany-Wnendt, P. 6
Poland 50
Poland, W. S. 74
Poznanski, E. O. 28
Proctor, R. 50
psychological border 2
Podell, D. 8
psychological DNA xi, 28

Rachman, A. W. 9
Rangell, L. 8, 74
Rapaport, D. 75
Read, A. 72
Redlich, F. xv

replacement child 28
Rosenfeld, D. 30–31
Rosenfeld, H. A. 30–31

Sabra 7
Schützenberger, A. A. 8
Searles, H. F. 93
Šebek, M. 12
second look 74
Sherich, I. 28
Sigmund Freud Center at Hebrew
    University 1, 4
Solnit, A. J. 28
Solyom, A. E. 28
Sonnenberg, S. M. 7
Sonntag, J. B. 6
splitting 5, 29–30, 74
    developmental splitting 26
Steinweis, A. G. 72
Stern, D. N. 26
Stern, J. 7
Stokes, P. 12
Stone, M. H. 25
Streeck-Fischer, A. 5
Stokes, P. 12
survivor syndrome 7

T4 euthanasia programme 49–51, 54,
    56, 58, 82, 98
Tähkä, V. 75, 78, 97
Target, M. xi
tattoo 17, 21 33, 36, 43, 52
therapeutic play 74–75
time collapse 13
transference xiii, 9, 32–33, 37, 39, 44,
    47, 74, 86–87
    built-in transference 85
transgenerational transmission xiii,
    7, 12, 53, 89, 95–96
trauma ix, xi, 6–9, 11, 13, 26, 30, 71, 74
    transmision of trauma x, 12, 34
Turkey xiv, 2

Van der Merwe, C. 6
Varvin, S. 12
Volkan, V. D. ix–xi, 2, 4–7, 11–13,
    24–25, 27–29, 31, 36, 45,
    74–75, 77–78, 85, 97

Waelder, A. 10
Weisberger, A. M. 4
Werman, D. S. 85

Wheelis, A. 73
Weisberger, A. 4
Winnicott, D. 2, 30

United States xiv, xiv, 1, 2, 6–8, 10, 12,
    71, 77, 80

Zintl, E. 11, 97

For Product Safety Concerns and Information please contact our EU representative GPSR@taylorandfrancis.com
Taylor & Francis Verlag GmbH, Kaufingerstraße 24, 80331 München, Germany

www.ingramcontent.com/pod-product-compliance
Lightning Source LLC
Chambersburg PA
CBHW051615230426
43668CB00013B/2122